Iceberg Down

Building High-Performance Teams

Iceberg Down

Building High-Performance Teams

Imagine Solving The Most Complex Problems

Ed Minnock

Published by Ed Minnock & Associates

Copyright © 2014 by Ed Minnock

All rights reserved. No part of this book may be reproduced in any form or by any electronic or mechanical means, including information storage and retrieval systems, without written permission from the author, except in the case of a reviewer, who may quote brief passages embodied in critical articles or in a review.

Trademarked names may appear throughout this book. Rather than use a trademark symbol with every occurrence of a trademarked name, names are used in an editorial fashion, with no intention of infringement of the respective owner's trademark.

The information in this book is distributed on an "as is" basis, without warranty. Although every precaution has been taken in the preparation of this work, neither the author nor the publisher shall have any liability to any person or entity with respect to any loss or damage caused or alleged to be caused directly or indirectly by the information contained in this book.

This is a work of fiction. Names, characters, places, and incidents either are the product of the author's imagination or are used fictitiously, and any resemblance to actual persons, living or dead, events, or locales is entirely coincidental.

This book is published by Ed Minnock & Associates. If your bookseller does not have this book in stock, or if you would like to order this book in quantity, please visit www.edminnockandassociates.com.

Cover design by Ed Minnock & Associates. Front cover image printed with permission from the National Oceanic and Atmospheric Administration/Department of Commerce. Photographer: Michael Van Woert.

All rights reserved.

ISBN-13: 978-1494433505
ISBN-10: 1494433508

Dedication

Jody and Killy

Contents

Acknowledgements	i
Introduction	1
Part I: Iceberg Down	
Chapter 1: Responsible Capitalist?	3
Chapter 2: Doing Our Job	6
Chapter 3: Hail the Savior	8
Chapter 4: Crack in the Armor	13
Chapter 5: Steady as She Goes	16
Chapter 6: If It's Successful, Do More	18
Chapter 7: An Old Friend	22
Chapter 8: Is the Issue Real?	26
Chapter 9: Does Anyone Care?	29
Chapter 10: Crossing the Rubicon	34
Chapter 11: Failure is Not an Option	41
Chapter 12: Someone Has to be Blamed	49
Chapter 13: Iceberg Down	51
Part I Summary	56
Part II: Learning to Succeed	
Chapter 14: The Road Back	59
Chapter 15: Too Good to Be True	62
Chapter 16: Learning to Succeed	70
Part II Summary	99
Part III: Transition	
Chapter 17: Habits Die Hard	103
Chapter 18: Experimentation	111
Chapter 19: Apocalypse Appears Certain	118

CONTENTS

Chapter 20: Pushing for Implementation	122
Chapter 21: Making It Visible	125
Chapter 22: Mad Emperor's Disease	134
Chapter 23: Had Enough	141
Part III Summary	143

Part IV: Defensive Versus Collaborative Responsibility

Chapter 24: Assumptions Drive Behavior	145
Chapter 25: A New Approach	150
Chapter 26: Those Prickly Issues	154
Chapter 27: Collaborative Responsibility	160
Part IV Summary	175

Part V: Collaborating Team

Chapter 28: Research	180
Chapter 29: Plussing It	184
Chapter 30: Team Building	190
Chapter 31: Dr. Hydrogen Bond Lurking Inside Us	204
Part V Summary	208

Epilogue: High-Performance Organization

Chapter 32: Decision Day	213
Chapter 33: High-Performance Organization	224
Epilogue Summary	240
Glossary	246
Notes	254
About the Author	257

Acknowledgments

I'd like to thank the many people who generously gave their time and effort to make the publication of *Iceberg Down* possible.

Thanks to the people who offered me opportunities to try different things, learn from those experiences, including countless mistakes, and try again. Thanks to the people on the various teams on which I worked. There were many great achievements.

In particular, thanks to Toni Holm, publisher of Word Keepers, for suggesting I use animal characters. Thanks to Steven H. Martin, publisher of Oaklea Press, for introducing me to *The Hero's Journey*, an approach to storytelling. Thanks to Marijke Jones for ideas and Dori Ransom for editing.

Thanks to family and friends for vital feedback: Chris Ray, Paul Beiser, Robbie Macbeth, Jeff Morrow, Michael Hering, and Joan Minnock.

Deep thanks to Robin Hering and Karen Gilleland for

ACKNOWLEDGEMENTS

meticulously dissecting every detail, which led to a better and more readable story.

Thanks to my daughter Killy for inspiration that made the story more interesting.

Finally, thanks to my beloved wife Jody for reliable feedback that kept me true to my purpose.

Introduction

This book presents a roadmap for resolving the complex problems found in business, education, government, non-profits, and communities.

Whether you are starting out in your career, an experienced professional or a highly-skilled specialist, the book will provide steps to transform yourself from a high-performing individual to an effective builder and leader of collaborative, high-performance teams.

You will learn the two pillars for building high-performance teams: collaboration tools and process, and collaborative responsibility. Collaboration tools and processes make problems and opportunities visible before, as well as after, important decisions are made. Collaborative responsibility means taking responsibility for the success of colleagues, as well as the success of the project.

The information you will work with is based on Lean, Agile Development, Six Sigma, learning cycles, and

INTRODUCTION

innovation-producing collaboration processes.

To drive home the relevancy and innovation-producing power of collaborative, high-performing teams, I have created a fictional story based upon a real problem: the critical shortage of fresh water in the world today.

Nearly 900 million people do not have access to clean water, and 2.5 billion people do not have a safe way to dispose of human waste. These conditions result in the death of nearly 10,000 people every day, mostly children under the age of five.[1] The ideas and techniques in *Iceberg Down* offer insight into resolving such highly complex problems.

In the story, icebergs are seen as the last chance to avoid a worldwide catastrophe. But harvesting water from icebergs is complicated, and time is running out. The main characters trying to solve the water crisis are penguins, and they don't get along very well, even though they try to do what's right.

The story describes how to overcome a myriad of interpersonal minefields that can paralyze teams, reduce organizational performance, and cause failure. The phrase "Iceberg Down" signals an emergency requiring immediate action.

You will learn, along with the penguins, how to build high-performance teams and how to help team members change their behavior so that others respond differently, more collaboratively. The contagious potential of high-performance teams makes collaborative behavior the lever that can move the world.

Can adversaries become a high-performance team in time to save the human race? The clock is ticking.

Part I: Iceberg Down

Chapter 1

Responsible Capitalist?

"You can't raise the price of water!" Colonel Tierney bellows from his chair in the cabin of his 200-foot yacht. "I've been apologizing for you all week. The UN is furious. Do you know how hard I worked to secure a no-bid contract with that organization?"

Dr. Hydrogen Bond, founder and CEO of Atlantis, and the most famous penguin in the world, calmly replies: "Humans are desperate for fresh water, and I have it, lots of it. It's simple supply and demand. You know how supply and demand works. You're an oil man."

"First of all, water is different. It's for poor people, and they can't pay high prices. Second, I'm an oil financier. And for the record, we in the oil industry could easily charge higher prices and make more profit. But we don't. And we're still raked over the coals."

"You're telling me the United Nations can't raise money for a slightly higher price of water?"

"You have to learn the difference between a responsible capitalist and a greedy scoundrel. Capitalism is a powerful force. Don't blow it."

"Okay, I won't raise the price of water. Besides, I have an idea that will produce more profit than you can imagine."

Colonel Tierney sits back with his arms folded. "I can imagine a lot of profit."

"Here's my idea: My water will save millions of humans from famine. I'll bet there are lots of rich humans who will pay handsomely to be a part of the greatest humanitarian achievement since germs were discovered. All we have to do is schedule the right event."

Colonel Tierney leans forward. "What do you have in mind?"

"I'm envisioning a celebration, the largest in history, right on the Atlantis iceberg, right in front of the lake filled with 35 billion gallons of the freshest water in the world."

"Tell me more."

"We invite Presidents, Prime Ministers, Kings and Queens, captains of industry, famous actors, entertainers, and your friends at the UN. Here's the kicker: Media companies will pay a fortune for filming rights."

A grin slowly spreads across Colonel Tierney's face. "The biggest celebration in history?"

"Bigger than the Olympics, and far more profitable."

"I like it. My investors will like it. My friends at the UN will certainly like rubbing elbows with the most powerful people in the world."

"Everybody wins, especially us. How's that for responsible capitalism?"

"You learn quickly. How soon can you pull off this

celebration? Aren't you draining the lake next week?"

"Draining can wait. Besides, the bigger the lake, the greater the value of my company."

Dr. Bond turns to leave.

"One more thing," Colonel Tierney says. "There's another oil industry lesson you might want to keep in mind."

"What's that?"

"Don't spill the merchandise."

Chapter 2

Doing Our Job

Standing on the iceberg, 100 feet above the ocean, Aqua Azure Penguin gazes across the vastness of the Great Atlantis Iceberg. The ten-miles-long and three-miles-wide iceberg contains an enormous, perfectly sculpted rectangular lake of fresh water, water that is destined to save millions of humans.

Aqua turns her back to the lake and peers into the distance. Suddenly she sees a twinkle a half-mile away. A small iceberg has broken off Atlantis, and it's directly in the path of a large cruise liner speeding toward Atlantis. Even from that distance, Aqua makes out the ship's name: "Commonwealth of Australia." Although the iceberg is small, it could sink the Prime Minister's ship.

Aqua shouts, "Iceberg Down!" All Atlantis employees know "Iceberg Down" means an emergency situation that requires immediate action.

Two orca whales pop out of the water. Aqua, the fastest swimmer at Atlantis, dives into the ocean and swims

IMAGINE SOLVING THE MOST COMPLEX PROBLEMS

like a rocket toward the small iceberg. The whales follow in her wake. When Aqua reaches the iceberg, she leaps out of the water and onto the iceberg. The two orca whales ram the iceberg, pushing it out of the way of the oncoming ship.

Exhausted and relieved, Aqua directs the whales to push the little iceberg back to Atlantis where her team of four penguins will freeze it to the side, the same way ice cubes freeze together in a cold glass of water.

Aqua was attracted to Atlantis because the company is providing an important service for humans, and the job is physically demanding. She can also practice her love of photography.

Aqua and her team are responsible for keeping the Atlantis iceberg positioned away from the shipping lanes and for rounding up small icebergs that break off. Although there have been several close calls, she is proud of her accident-free record.

Chapter 3

Hail the Savior

With the rogue iceberg secure, Aqua and her team walk up the steps they built on the side of the Atlantis iceberg to join a company-wide communication meeting called by Dr. Hydrogen Bond, Chief Executive Officer and founder of Atlantis.

The meeting is taking place between the lake and the palatial main building. Chrystal Hexagon Penguin, Vice President of Public Relations, addresses the audience.

"Good morning." Chrystal pauses and scans the crowd of penguins who work for Atlantis. The majority are architects, engineers, and craftsmen who design, build, and maintain the topside of the iceberg. Aqua and her team stand in the back.

Chrystal continues: "We, the executive team at Atlantis, want to thank you. We have created an enormous lake by melting the top of this iceberg. It's the freshest water in the world. We have also erected castles, offices, and statues, all made with ice from heavy water. Heavy water melts at thirty-nine degrees, so the beauty you see before you will hardly melt now that we are in late autumn. Dr. Bond invented the world's best process for producing heavy water: water made from deuterium instead of hydrogen. As many of you know, deuterium's nucleus has a neutron and a proton, while the normal hydrogen nucleus has only a proton."

Crystal gazes at the magnificent iceberg. "This week's announcements: We have five new yachts on the lake. The video you've all been waiting for, 'The Life and Times of Dr. Hydrogen Bond' is in the Atlantis Gift Store. Finally, we are celebrating the grand opening of the Casino Bond. You will see many of our human guests gambling, eating meals, and drinking cocktails. All the ice cubes served at Casino Bond have just enough heavy water in them to sink to the bottom of the glass. A cool trick, I'm sure you'll agree."

A few penguins laugh.

Crystal pauses and smiles. "I'd like to introduce the Chief Executive Officer and founder of Atlantis. Here he is: the penguin whose vision you see before you, Dr. Bond, Dr. Hydrogen Bond!"

The penguins cheer as Dr. Bond jogs up to the podium and takes the microphone. He gazes upon his masterpiece and smiles. He is a handsome penguin with a large head and long beak.

"We have a date with destiny!" Dr. Bond announces. His deep voice commands attention. "Thanks to you, we are achieving a feat far greater than ourselves!"

He pauses. "Here we are off the coast of Melbourne, Australia, where the ocean water is cold enough that the underwater portion of the iceberg has hardly melted at all, but the top has melted rapidly during the warm summer and has continued to melt during a very warm autumn."

He pauses and continues in a serious tone: "Humans face a water crisis of enormous proportion. Two-and-a-half billion humans lack fresh water.[1] Many are dying. Unlike us, humans can't drink ocean water. Human water must be clean and almost free of salt."

Dr. Bond holds a document in the air. "I am holding a contract with the United Nations for the sale of every ounce of water in this lake. Within weeks, millions of desperate families will have a reliable supply of fresh water."

His smile broadens. "On this iceberg, we have rebuilt the lost city of Atlantis. Our floating paradise is being compared to the greatest human-made structures in history: The Pyramids of Egypt, the Great Wall of China, and the Taj Mahal of India. You are all part of the greatest achievement in penguin history!"

Applause and cheers. "Today is a very special day. My business partner Colonel Tierney and I have decided to create lakes of fresh water on ten new icebergs. We will start immediately and complete the project in one year. Now, please welcome Colonel Tierney, my partner and Atlantis' largest investor."

Colonel Tierney makes his way to the podium using an ornately carved wooden cane to secure his footing on the ice.

Colonel Tierney gazes at the lake, the statues, and the Casino Bond. "I've spent my whole life investing in great companies. But Atlantis is the greatest company I've ever invested in. Dr. Bond has developed the perfect synergistic strategy. By melting the top of this iceberg, Atlantis will provide an essential service to humans. By building a resort, Atlantis is making lots of money. Without the lake, there would be little interest in the resort. Without the resort, there would be little return on investment. Dr. Bond is a visionary who doesn't take no for an answer."

Colonel Tierney stops to take a drink of water. "I just drank water from the lake, and it's the best water I've ever tasted. But I'm not used to ice cubes that sink."

Dr. Bond takes the microphone. "Thank you, Colonel Tierney."

Dr. Bond points to two flagpoles made of ice from heavy water, and a large banner drops. It reads, "Fresh Water for Every Human".

Crystal walks quickly to the microphone. "This is our vision, 'Fresh Water for Every Human.' We have made buttons for every Atlantis employee. Please pick one up in the lobby and wear it proudly." She attaches a button to her chest and hands one to Dr. Bond, who does the same.

"Thank you, Crystal. Now we have a very special guest. Let me introduce Peter Crittenden, the Prime Minister of Australia." A tall man of about forty, with thick black hair walks gingerly on the ice to the podium, slipping here and there as he goes.

"Good day," Peter Crittenden says. "What you have accomplished is of great importance to me and my country. It is an honor for the Great Atlantis Iceberg to be stationed off the coast of Australia."

He pauses. "Australia has been suffering through a terrible drought. Millions of Australians don't have enough water. Food prices have soared. Normally, high food prices create profits for farmers that can be reinvested to increase output, but not when high food prices are caused by lack of fresh water. Farmers are losing money and customers cannot pay the higher prices. Everybody loses. We desperately need fresh water to nourish people and prevent disease. It is with great anticipation that I look forward to receiving the first shipment of water. I and all Australians thank you."

The penguins applaud and congratulate each other as they drift back to their work areas.

Chapter 4

Crack in the Armor

The workday is over, and most penguins have gone back to their apartments or off to dinner. Aqua walks briskly back to the maintenance office to suit up for her weekly inspection of the underside of the iceberg. Frostbite, a new member of her team, is pouring over data.

"Are you doing experiments again tonight?" Aqua asks.

"As always. I'm collecting real-time data to evaluate a mathematical model I created in college for ice melting."

"Does the data correlate?"

"Yes, fairly closely. You know that energy is required to melt the top of the iceberg. The energy comes from sunlight and the warmth of the air. The sun is the dominant factor, and the fact that this summer was hotter than average explains why the lake is so much larger than planned."

Aqua pulls on her oxygen tanks.

"Are you swimming underneath?" Frostbite asks.

"Yep, I'm doing my weekly check of the underside. I look for ice about to break off so we can catch it before it does. It's boring, but I like the swim."

"Mind if I join you?"

"Be my guest. Have you ever been underside?"

"No, but I'd like to see it."

As Frostbite retrieves his oxygen tanks, Aqua watches the flat screen TV on the wall.

"Welcome to today's Water Report," the announcer says. "I'm Walter Penguin. In our top story, Dr. Hydrogen Bond, CEO of Atlantis, announced today that Atlantis will build ten more fresh water lakes on icebergs in one year. According to Dr. Bond, these additional icebergs will fulfill his vision of providing fresh water for every human.

In a related story, a water crisis is developing in the Middle East. It is a region with little rainfall, but the population has tripled in the last thirty years. Last winter's precipitation was far below normal. Although Middle Eastern countries have made large investments in desalination, the facilities are coming on line too slowly. It looks as if Dr. Bond's fresh water will arrive just in time. And that's the way it is. I'm Walter Penguin with the Water Report."

Frostbite groans as he hoists the heavy oxygen tanks up and over his head.

"Need help?" Aqua asks.

Frostbite is ambitious, but inexperienced. He joined Atlantis a month ago, right out of college.

"I got it," he says, as the strap catches under his beak and nearly chokes him.

"Here," Aqua chuckles and lifts the tank so he can properly strap on the oxygen.

IMAGINE SOLVING THE MOST COMPLEX PROBLEMS

"These tanks are heavy," Frostbite says, as they walk toward the slide on the north side of the iceberg.

"Follow me," Aqua shouts, as she slides belly-down into the water. Frostbite follows. They swim nine hundred feet straight down to the bottom of the iceberg and then make their way underneath.

The two penguins turn on the lights on the front of their helmets and breathe oxygen every few minutes. Aqua looks back and sees Frostbite falling behind. She slows down.

Aqua swims her usual zigzag pattern from north to south as Frostbite follows. Suddenly she stops and gasps. Frostbite swims up next to her. Directly in front of them is a large crevice, over a hundred feet long and twenty feet across. Aqua and Frostbite swim thirty feet up into the fissure and inspect every inch. She motions for Frostbite to serve as a gauge while she takes pictures with her waterproof camera.

They swim back to the surface and walk up the stairs and back to the maintenance office. Aqua sends an urgent e-mail to her boss, Celsius Kelvin Penguin, requesting a meeting first thing in the morning.

Chapter 5

Steady as She Goes

Aqua enters Celsius' modest office with a desk, a guest table with two chairs, and a small window in back of the desk. On the wall is a poster that reads,

> *"Act quickly and do the right thing, and if that doesn't work, act quickly and do something. But don't do nothing!"*
> *Dr. Hydrogen Bond*

Celsius Penguin joined Atlantis a year ago, just a few weeks before Aqua. A month later, he was promoted to Director of Operations, reporting directly to Dr. Bond.

"Good morning," Aqua says, entering Celsius' office.

"Good job yesterday on that iceberg," Celsius replies. "We would not want a piece of ice from Atlantis to sink the Prime Minister's boat."

Aqua joins Celsius at the guest table. Aqua explains what she found and shows him the pictures on her laptop.

"You know the lake is 40 percent larger than planned," Aqua says. "I suspect water may be seeping into the ice under the lake and weakening it to the point where the weight of the water is causing the crack."

Celsius studies the pictures carefully. "Are you sure this crack is new?"

"I check the underside every week. I could not have missed it."

"I doubt it's serious. Dr. Bond selected this iceberg because it's very strong. Besides, we start draining the lake next week. When the lake is drained, we can do a thorough inspection of the lake bottom, but I think we'll be all right."

"Do you want updates? I plan to inspect the crack every day to see if it's growing."

"Don't forget your number one responsibility is to prevent rogue icebergs from hitting ships. It's going to be very busy around here."

Aqua leaves his office feeling a sense of frustration. She thought Celsius would be more interested in the crack under the lake.

Chapter 6

If It's Successful, Do More

One Week Later

Aqua checks her watch. Celsius' staff meeting starts in a few minutes. She swims to the surface, climbs the stairs, and walks swiftly to the main office building. She doesn't have time to drop off her oxygen tanks at the maintenance office, so she carries them with her.

The conference room is down the hall from the lobby on the first floor of the company headquarters. The building is made entirely of ice from heavy water and cooled to thirty-two degrees. The lobby is supported by gothic arches and a parade of ice statues.

As Aqua approaches the conference room, she hears applause and laughter. Dr. Bond and Crystal Penguin are there along with Celsius and his staff. Everyone is wearing "Fresh Water for Every Human" buttons. Everyone except Aqua.

Aqua enters the windowless conference room. She places her oxygen tanks in the corner and stands in the

IMAGINE SOLVING THE MOST COMPLEX PROBLEMS

doorway.

Dr. Bond is standing next to Celsius. "As our new Vice President of Operations and newest senior executive, Celsius will be responsible for operations on all icebergs, including the ten new icebergs. My congratulations to Celsius for a job well done."

Applause.

Dr. Bond continues: "We are going to be very busy during the next few weeks. Celsius will fill you in on the details. Most of all, I want to thank you for your hard work. Things are going amazingly well. Now, if you will excuse me, I have a meeting with an important customer."

Dr. Bond and Crystal leave.

All the penguins sit down. Aqua chooses a chair at the end of the conference table made of ice from heavy water.

"Let's get started," Celsius says. "I, too, have an organizational announcement. Nitro Penguin has been named Operations Manager for one of the new icebergs. Nitro has been with Atlantis since the beginning and is our top explosives and ice-carving expert. Please congratulate Nitro."

All the penguins cheer. Nitro smiles.

Celsius continues: "Dr. Bond is thrilled with our progress. Three months ago we reached our goal of twenty-five billion gallons of fresh water. We now have thirty-five billion, and all of it is sold. We are selling lake time on our yachts for a million dollars a week, and we're back ordered. Our iceberg has been visited by heads of state, royalty, and famous actors. Television networks are paying a fortune for the chance to film up close. We are on track to make far more money than planned."

"I have a question," Aqua says. "With so many humans

desperate for water, who decides which countries will get water first?"

"Good question. Because the Middle East is in a crisis situation, Dr. Bond has decided that the first shipments of water will go to Middle Eastern countries. Australia will be second."

Celsius checks his notes. "Oh yes. How could I forget? Dr. Bond decided to postpone draining the lake for five weeks. In four weeks we are having the greatest celebration in history. We are inviting dignitaries from around the world. The celebration will be televised in every country. It will be bigger than the Olympics."

"How are we going to secure the lake?" Aqua worries that the lake won't last that long at the rate the crevice is growing.

"Dr. Bond wants to raise the banks so the lake can hold more water."

"Is that a good idea? The lake is already 40 percent bigger than planned. Shouldn't we be draining the lake to relieve the pressure?"

"Dr. Bond does not want to lose any fresh water," Celsius says, ignoring her question. "We have more orders for fresh water than we can fill. We're also going to build more ice sculptures and ice castles from heavy water, and we're going to build an addition onto the Casino Bond so we can accommodate more guests. If your teams need to work overtime, consider it preapproved by Dr. Bond."

Celsius looks around the room. "Nitro and I will be traveling to the Ross Ice Shelf right after this meeting to find ten icebergs suitable for lakes of fresh water. Because I'll be gone, there will not be a staff meeting next week. Now let's get to work. We have a lot to do and not much time to do it."

As the others file out of the room, Aqua stays seated. She feels as though she was run over by a whale. The crack under the lake is growing, and the lake will not be drained for another five weeks. She rests her head on the table.

"Excuse me," Crystal Penguin says from the doorway. "I have this room reserved."

Aqua turns and sees Crystal with six well-groomed penguins from the Marketing Department, all wearing their "Fresh Water for Every Human" buttons.

"Sorry," she says and picks up her oxygen tanks and camera and heads out the door.

As Aqua passes the group, one says, "They need to give those operations penguins some rest."

Chapter 7

An Old Friend

Aqua walks through the lobby. Humans are everywhere: Gambling in the Casino Bond, taking pictures of ice sculptures, and shopping in the Atlantis Gift Store. She navigates through the crowd and walks outside.

"Aqua," a familiar voice rings out. She turns and recognizes Aristotle Penguin. She hasn't seen him since college.

"Aristotle, it's nice to see you. What have you been up to?"

"It's great to see you too, Aqua. Well... after graduating, I started a company that makes fresh water in Renaissance Village in Antarctica. It's called Glacier Fresh Water. We melt water from a glacier just before it enters the ocean. It's a small operation. I can see from your badge that you work here."

"Yes, for about a year."

"Did I hear that you swam around Antarctica?"

"I did. It was an incredible experience; I explored every sea cave, glacier, and saw thousands of fish. I took hundreds of pictures, including fish thought to be extinct."

"I'll bet that experience helped you land your job at Atlantis."

"It did." Aqua remembers that she had been told a degree was required. The company waived the requirement because of her swim around Antarctica.

"What do you do here?"

"I lead the team responsible for keeping the Atlantis iceberg properly positioned and away from shipping lanes. We also make sure no little icebergs that break off Atlantis are hit by boats. We've never had an accident."

"Congratulations. Are those oxygen tanks?"

"Yes. Sometimes I swim under the iceberg to check on its overall integrity."

"Well, it was great seeing you. If you're ever near Renaissance Village, look me up."

"I'll do that."

Aristotle turns to walk away.

Aqua remembers Aristotle's encouragement during college. He was like a father to her and many others at Penguin University. Even though she didn't graduate, she would never have made it as far as she did without his encouragement.

"Aristotle," Aqua says, walking briskly to catch up to him. "I'd like your advice on something."

"Sure."

"Let's walk." Aqua moves toward the lake and away from the crowd. "What I'm going to tell you is confidential. You have to promise not to tell anyone."

"You know me, Aqua. You have my word."

"Thanks. When I was making my weekly inspection of the underside of the iceberg, I found a crack. I took pictures and showed them to my boss. He told me not to worry because the lake was to be drained this week. I just learned that the lake will not be drained for five weeks. The lake is already 40 percent larger than planned, and I've been measuring the crack every day. It's growing. Nobody seems to care. I don't know what to do."

"Where exactly is the crack?"

"It's directly under the lake near the south side. It runs north and south."

"How thick is the ice where the crack is?"

"It's hard to tell. From the top of the crack to the lakebed, I'd say 600 feet, but lake water may be seeping into the lakebed and weakening the ice. I've been on the bottom of the lake, and it's all slush. There is no telling how strong the ice is at this point."

"What did your boss say?"

"He doesn't think it's a problem."

"Does he have a good reason for thinking it's not a problem?"

"He said Dr. Bond selected this iceberg because it's very strong."

"What's the risk?"

"Fresh water may leak into the ocean or…" Aqua pauses.

"Or what?"

"The crack grows. The iceberg weakens. Then it breaks, and all the fresh water spills into the ocean. Yachts sucked into the ocean. Humans and penguins crushed by water and ice. No fresh water for humans."

Aristotle's smile vanishes. "That's serious. I'd suggest

IMAGINE SOLVING THE MOST COMPLEX PROBLEMS

you try to find out for sure what jeopardy the iceberg is in. If your concern is real, Dr. Bond needs to know. And you don't want to take the issue to the CEO without strong evidence."

Aqua stares at the lake and thinks, *"I'm going to have to find out how strong the ice is under the lake."*

"Also, listen carefully to what others say and try to understand them. It's a natural defense mechanism to defend our position and press our points. However, we learn by listening and understanding those who disagree with us. It's hard and it takes practice."

"Good idea. Any other suggestions?"

"Give others time to absorb the situation. Not everyone figures things out as fast as you do. Good luck."

Chapter 8

Is the Issue Real?

"Are you going under the iceberg again?" Frostbite asks as Aqua puts on her oxygen tanks.

"Yes. I'm going to take samples of ice from the bottom of the iceberg and from the bottom of the lake. I'm trying to find out how strong the iceberg is under the lake. I want to know if the crack is caused by weak ice."

"Can I help?"

"You sure can."

The two of them swim under the iceberg and cut off large chunks of ice with hammers and chisels in a dozen places directly under the lake. They use pulleys to hoist the ice to the top of the iceberg, where they place it on a sled and pull it to the lab.

Frostbite cuts a square prism out of the ice. All angles of a square prism are ninety degrees. Two of the three sides are same length. The cross-sectional area is six inches by six inches, and the length is eighteen inches.

IMAGINE SOLVING THE MOST COMPLEX PROBLEMS

Frostbite drills holes and places metal rods in the ice. He then places a force gauge between the posts and applies pressure. "I'm at 150 pounds of pressure. It hasn't broken yet. This is blue ice. It's solid."

"That's what I expected," Aqua says. "This ice is probably fifteen thousand years old. Pressure from a thousand feet of snow melted the snow and refroze it into very solid ice. It would have to be under tremendous pressure to crack. Let's see what's on the bottom of the lake."

Aqua and Frostbite swim down a hundred feet to the bottom of the lake. They don't need the chisels and hammers they brought with them because the bottom of the lake is complete slush. They return to the maintenance office and retrieve two ten-feet-long metal poles, which they plan to drive through the slush in order to find solid ice.

Aqua and Frostbite return to the bottom of the lake. On the north side they find solid ice five feet below the slush. They dig through the slush with shovels, and chop off large pieces of ice and haul them back to the freezer.

"This ice is entirely different," Frostbite says. "Fifty pounds of force breaks it in two."

"The granules are large, which means the ice is weak," Aqua says, examining a piece under a microscope. "I need to know what the ice looks like under the south side of the lake, right over the crack at the deepest point."

"That's nearly two hundred feet deep."

Aqua nods agreement. Aqua and Frostbite tie five ten-feet-long metal poles together, and drive the poles through the slush on the south side until they reach solid ice. The slush is forty-five feet thick.

"Let's build a tunnel," Aqua says. "We need to find a pipe large enough for us to fit inside and long enough to reach the ice under the slush. Then we'll drive the pipe through the slush, and swim down through the pipe and retrieve the ice samples."

They search behind the maintenance office for pipe.

"I can fit in this one," Frostbite says as he wiggles his way in.

"I'll never get in there," Aqua says.

"No problem. I'll get the samples."

"This is dangerous work. If the pipe moves, you could become trapped under the slush."

They can't find a larger pipe.

"It looks like it's up to me," Frostbite says. "Don't worry, Aqua, I'll be careful."

Aqua and Frostbite weld large pipes together and place a cap on the end that can be removed from the inside. With help from other penguins, they roll it into the lake and drive it down through the slush.

Frostbite swims into the pipe and down toward the ice. An hour later he reappears with a fifty-pound piece of ice. Using a sled, they haul the ice to the lab.

"These granules are three times as big," Aqua announces, "which means the tensile strength should be one ninth as much."

"This ice practically falls apart," Frostbite says.

Aqua inspects several pieces under a microscope. "That's because the ice is full of liquid water."

Aqua and Frostbite look at each piece.

Aqua says, "The crack under the lake is caused by lake water seeping into the ice and weakening the iceberg. Once liquid water gets into the ice, the ice loses its strength."

Chapter 9

Does Anyone Care?

Aqua arrives early for Celsius' staff meeting carrying a cooler and a backpack. She takes a seat at the end of the conference-room table. She wears a "Fresh Water for Every Human" button for the first time. Celsius arrives a few minutes later.

"You're early," Celsius says.

"How was your trip?"

"Excellent and exhausting. We found five perfect icebergs. We're going back right after the celebration for five more. We arrived at three this morning. I never dreamed this business would become so big so fast."

Celsius sits at the other end of the table as the rest of his staff files in.

"Let's get started," Celsius says. "First, Dr. Bond and I want to thank you all for your hard work over the last two weeks. We're almost ready for the celebration. Hundreds of the world's most important penguins and humans will be here, along with the world's largest media networks."

ICEBERG DOWN: BUILDING HIGH-PERFORMANCE TEAMS

Celsius' tone turns serious. "That's the good news. The bad news is, we don't have enough dock capacity to handle all the yachts, cruise ships, and boats. We don't want dignitaries waiting to dock their yacht. So we're going to build a dock on the south side of the iceberg, right next to the lake. First, we need to cut away some underwater ice. Nitro, can you show us the plan?"

Nitro stands and spreads a drawing out on the table. "Here is the lake, and here is the underwater portion of the iceberg that we're going to cut. It's directly south of the lake and juts out by twenty to thirty feet. We're going to cut the ice flush with the topside, so the yachts can dock right up against the iceberg without danger of hitting underwater ice."

He points to a red line showing where the iceberg will be cut. "The ice is fairly thin so we'll use small explosives. This is a relatively minor job. You'll feel a slight vibration if you're standing nearby. My team will mark the detonation points, drill holes along this line, and perform the detonation. No one will be allowed to swim near the detonation site. Any questions?"

"Yes," Aqua says. "There is large crack under the south side of the lake very near the ice you plan to detonate. That ice provides structural support to the underside of the iceberg. It acts as a brace. The melting ice and huge lake have redistributed the weight of the iceberg from the ends to the middle. One cubic yard of water weighs nearly a ton. If we remove the brace, we increase the risk that the iceberg will fracture underneath the lake. If that happens, all the water will spill into the ocean."

The room hangs in silence.

Aqua continues, "Can the dock be located somewhere

else, away from the lake?"

"No," Celsius states. "Dr. Bond has decided to build the dock on the south side of the lake so the first thing dignitaries see when they climb onto the iceberg is the magnificent lake."

Aqua stands up and leans on the table. "But the ice under the lake is under enormous stress due to the weight of the water."

"What are you talking about?" Nitro says. "The iceberg is 900 feet thick."

"The lake over the crack is almost 200 feet deep, and the crack extends 100 feet up. That leaves 600 feet of ice."

"Do you know how strong ice is?" Nitro shoots back. "A foot of ice can support a ten-ton truck. We have 600 feet of ice. This iceberg could support a mountain."

Aqua bites her tongue, remembering what Aristotle told her. She sits back down in her chair.

"I agree with you if we have blue ice," she says. "But the problem is that the lake water has seeped into the ice on the bottom of the lake and weakened the iceberg."

"You think 600 feet of ice is going to melt in a couple of weeks?" Nitro responds. "We start full-scale pumping in three weeks."

Nitro looks to Celsius for help.

"The decision to cut the ice has been made. Our job is to carry out that decision."

"You're not listening," Aqua pleads. "The ice under the lake is filled with water. It has no tensile strength. It practically falls apart. Remember, the lake is 40 percent larger than planned, and we were supposed to drain it two weeks ago."

"Do you have proof that the iceberg is at risk?" Celsius

asks.

"Yes, I have proof. I have pictures of the crack, and I have samples of the ice under the lake."

Aqua retrieves her digital camera from her backpack and connects it to the projector. "Here is the crack three weeks ago." Aqua takes a deep breath. "This is two weeks ago. This is last week, and this is today."

She pauses to let the images sink in.

"I have ice samples also." She places the cooler on the conference room table and opens it. "The ice is labeled. Here is the test data that shows the tensile strength of the ice from the bottom of the iceberg and under the lake. As you can see, the ice under the south side of the lake is so weak it almost falls apart."

Celsius picks up the weak ice as Aqua continues. "I suggest we meet with Dr. Bond and show him these photos and samples. We need to convince him not to detonate that ice and to start draining the lake immediately. We have accomplished too much to risk losing everything."

Celsius nods. "I'll talk to Dr. Bond before we detonate the ice. Please send me your pictures and test data."

Celsius glances at his watch. "There is no staff meeting next week. I'm with Dr. Bond all day. He wants to review the status of all our projects."

"Is there anything we can do to help?" Aqua asks.

"Make sure everything is on or ahead of schedule. He doesn't tolerate missed schedules or excuses. Now, if you'll excuse me, I have another meeting." He quickly leaves.

Aqua follows Celsius out of the conference room, down the hallway, and into his office. Celsius turns and sees her standing there.

"Celsius," Aqua says, searching for the right words, "I would like to present the evidence to Dr. Bond."

"Why?"

"So I can answer any questions he may have."

"That won't be necessary."

"I believe it's important that Dr. Bond understand the gravity of the situation!"

"I will make sure Dr. Bond understands the gravity. Thank you. Please send me the images."

Celsius walks out of his office, leaving Aqua standing alone.

Chapter 10

Crossing the Rubicon

Next Morning, 7:30 a.m.

"Aqua!" Celsius' voice screams out of Aqua's phone and into her ear, interrupting her team meeting. "Nitro detonated the ice. There are large pieces of ice headed toward a ship. It's an Iceberg Down situation."

"What! I thought you were going to talk to Dr. Bond."

"I did. He said detonate. I need you to round up the ice before ships start sinking!"

Aqua and her team race toward the detonation area. Nitro is standing on the edge of the iceberg waiving frantically at a 30-foot yacht dangerously close to several large pieces of ice.

Upon seeing Nitro waving, the yacht captain turns the yacht toward the iceberg and directly toward a large piece of ice.

Aqua and her team arrive at the edge of the iceberg.

Aqua yells, "Stop sign."

Instantly, Aqua stands sideways and curls her body into

the shape of an "S". Frostbite faces forward, with his feet together and fins extended straight out to each side to form a "T". Two other team members join fins and form an "O". The last member curls forward to form a "P".

The yacht cuts its engine. It slows quickly. But before the yacht can stop, it collides with the piece of ice.

Aqua dives into the ocean and races to the ship. Upon reaching the ship, she waives to the captain and dives underwater. Aqua finds a dent in the hull but no puncture. The yacht is sea-worthy but in need of repair.

Aqua returns to the surface and asks permission to board. The captain consents. Aqua climbs on-board and introduces herself. She tells the captain that she will take pictures of the damage. She also tells him Atlantis will pay for repairs. She records his name and contact information in her waterproof phone.

Within minutes, Aqua's team clears the area with the help of two orca whales. The yacht starts its engine and chugs away.

Aqua walks back to the maintenance office to file an accident report. She logs into the employee portal, and finds that it has been updated with a new software release. She's begins to fill in the required fields. Without warning, the system kicks her out. She logs in again. Again, the system kicks her out. After five unsuccessful tries, she drafts an accident reports with pen and paper, prints out a picture of the dent, makes a copy, and carries the original to the administration department.

Aqua returns to the maintenance office, climbs into her oxygen tanks and swims under the iceberg to inspect the crack. Her jaw drops. The crack is two thousand feet long, fifty feet across, and a hundred feet up. Aqua inspects the crack and takes pictures.

When Aqua returns topside, her phone beeps. She has a message from Celsius asking her to report to his office immediately. The message was left an hour ago. Apparently, her phone doesn't work under the iceberg.

Aqua approaches Celsius' office and stands in the doorway. Celsius and Nitro are sitting at Celsius' guest table talking.

"Dr. Bond wants a plan to build ten lakes on ten icebergs with resorts in one year," Celsius says.

"I don't see how that is possible," Nitro says. "Three years were required to build Atlantis."

Celsius sees Aqua in the doorway. "Aqua! Where have you been? I called you over an hour ago."

"After we cleared the ice from the detonation area, I went under the iceberg to inspect the crack under the lake. My phone doesn't work under the iceberg."

"Dr. Bond heard about the accident with the yacht. He's furious. He wants to know why the detonation area wasn't quarantined." Celsius and Nitro stare at Aqua.

"The detonation area wasn't quarantined because nobody told me the ice was being detonated first thing this morning." Aqua looks at Nitro.

"It was a small job. I didn't expect any boats around the iceberg that early."

"Who told Dr. Bond about the accident with the yacht?" Celsius demands.

"I wrote up an accident report on paper because the employee portal wasn't working. I dropped it off at the administration department. Maybe someone took it to Dr. Bond's office."

Celsius shakes his head. "I do not want Dr. Bond

finding out about accidents before I do. From now on, bring accident reports to me." Celsius rubs his forehead. "We have to start working as a team. You two have to talk to each other, and you have to keep me in the loop."

Nitro looks at Celsius. "What are you going to tell Dr. Bond?"

"I'll think of something."

"*He's going to blame me*," Aqua says to herself.

"Next topic," Celsius barks. "As soon as we finish draining the lake, Dr. Bond wants the Atlantis iceberg pushed north, just off the coast of Sydney. We have more orders for fresh water than we can fill. Dr. Bond says we can deliver another 10 billion gallons during the winter because it's warmer in Sydney. Aqua, can you round up enough whales to push the iceberg to Sydney?"

Aqua stares at him.

"Can you round up the whales?"

"Yes."

"Good. Dr. Bond wants the iceberg moved as soon as the lake is drained – as in the following day."

Aqua remains standing in the doorway.

"Is there anything else?" Celsius asks.

"Um, yes. The crack under the iceberg is larger. It's 2,000 feet long, 50 feet across, and a 100 feet up. I'm worried about the structural integrity of the ice under the lake, particularly since the ice on the south side has been detonated. If we drain the lake from both sides, we should be able to drain a third in the next ten days. We'll still have a huge lake for the celebration. We can tell the media we drained it to deliver fresh water to humans faster. Draining the lake is a win-win proposition."

Celsius shakes his head. "Between now and the

celebration? Are you nuts? Dr. Bond is receiving some of the most important humans and penguins in the world: Presidents, Prime Ministers, Kings and Queens. And you want to line Atlantis with tankers? I can see it now: pumps screaming, tankers bellowing black plumes of diesel exhaust, dignitaries coughing and wheezing."

Nitro laughs.

Celsius continues: "As soon as the celebration is over, the iceberg will be off-limits to media and visitors. We will line each side with the world's largest tankers and drain the lake as fast as possible."

Nitro adds: "We have a date with destiny. We have to stick to the plan."

"You should see these pictures," Aqua says, pulling out her camera. "I'd like to show the latest pictures to Dr. Bond. He needs to understand the risk we're facing."

"Dr. Bond is confident the iceberg won't break. Your job is to make sure the iceberg is positioned properly and that no boats are sunk by ice that breaks off Atlantis. We can't afford any more accidents. Can you do that, or do I have to ask someone else?!"

"Yes," Aqua replies softly.

"Another thing, don't tell anyone else about the crack. We don't want rumors flying around. Now is there anything else?"

"I'll send you these images."

As Aqua turns to leave, she overhears Celsius and Nitro.

"Where were we?" Celsius asks.

"The plan to build ten Atlantis-like icebergs in one year, even though it's not possible," Nitro says.

"I don't think building ten Atlantis-like icebergs in one

IMAGINE SOLVING THE MOST COMPLEX PROBLEMS

year is possible either, but I am not going to tell Dr. Bond it can't be done. He doesn't tolerate excuses."

"I know. He wants results."

Aqua walks slowly toward the lobby. *They're living in a fantasy land. We have a giant crack under the lake that is growing rapidly. This iceberg is at risk of breaking, and they're dreaming up plans to build ten more.*

She navigates through the lobby and outside. Then she stops. *Dr. Bond has to know what's going on.* She turns around and walks briskly up the stairs to Dr. Bond's office suite. She takes a deep breath and enters.

His office suite looks like a museum. Statues line the walls. A large desk rests squarely in the middle of the room. His assistant, Jewel Penguin, is on the phone. Behind her are two ten-foot-tall stained-ice double doors, the entry into Dr. Bond's office.

Aqua watches the flat screen TV on the wall in front of Jewel's desk. "And now, the daily Water Report," it drones. "Good afternoon. I'm Walter Penguin with the water report. An emergency is developing in the Middle East. While we are entering winter, the northern hemisphere is entering summer. The rainy season is over, and the entire region is experiencing the worst drought ever recorded. As a result, Dr. Hydrogen Bond, the CEO of Atlantis, announced today that the Middle East, not Australia, will receive the first delivery of water from Atlantis."

"May I help you?" Jewel asks in a loud and raspy voice.

"Um, yes," Aqua says, taking a step back. "I would like an appointment with Dr. Bond."

"What is the topic?"

"Topic?" Aqua thinks for a minute. "The topic is the crack under the lake."

"Let's see," Jewel says. "Dr. Bond is very busy. How about next Friday at 4:45?"

"That's only three days before the celebration," Aqua says, knowing there would be little time to drain any water from the lake. "Please, this is urgent. Would it be possible to meet earlier?"

"Let's see. "If I move some appointments, you can meet with him at 8:15 tomorrow morning."

"Thank you."

"Don't be late."

"I won't."

Chapter 11

Failure is Not an Option

"You went over Celsius' head and made an appointment with Dr. Bond!" Frostbite exclaims.

"We may have created a doomsday device here," Aqua says. "Dr. Bond needs to know what the risk is, and Celsius isn't telling him. I put together an open-and-shut case to convince Dr. Bond to drain the lake to a safe level."

"Do you know what a safe level is?"

"I think 30 billion gallons should be safe."

"Is there time before the celebration?"

"I talked to the Purchasing Department. If Dr. Bond pulls some strings, we can drain the lake down to thirty billion gallons by Sunday noon and the tankers will all be gone by Monday."

"Do you think Dr. Bond will go for it?"

"How can he argue against draining the lake when he sees how large the crack is and how weak the ice is under the south side? We've got to take pressure off the crack."

Aqua and Frostbite sip fresh water from the lake that is provided to all employees.

"I really don't like fresh water," Frostbite says. "What are you going to show Dr. Bond?"

"Last night I made large pictures of everything. I'm going to line them up so Dr. Bond can see them all at once. I'm also bringing ice samples from under the lake. That way he can see how fast the crack is growing and how weak the ice is under the lake."

"Good luck."

"Thanks for all your help." Aqua gathers her presentation material and the cooler.

"Aqua, you forgot your 'Fresh Water for Every Human' button'."

"Actually, I lost it."

"Here, take mine."

"Thanks. Now I'm politically correct."

Aqua walks through the lobby and up the stairs to Dr. Bond's office.

"Good morning," Aqua says as she approaches Jewel's desk. "I have an appointment with Dr. Bond."

"Yes, of course. He's running a few minutes late. Please have a seat."

Aqua sits. She notices a large banner just under the large flat screen TV that says, "Fresh Water for Every Human". Good thing she has the button on. Aqua watches the Penguin News.

"We have a breaking news story," the announcer says. "A reliable source has reported that the Atlantis iceberg is in jeopardy because of a large crack directly under the giant lake of fresh water."

Aqua's heart skips a beat.

"I dislike the news media more every day," Jewel says. "They'll do anything for a story, even if it means lying."

"I'm curious," Aqua says. "Do you know why Dr. Bond is named Hydrogen Bond? He's the only penguin whose last name isn't penguin."

"His name is Dr. Hydrogen Bond because hydrogen bonds are the most important phenomena in the natural world, and he is the most important penguin in the whole world. Hydrogen bonds are the reason water freezes and boils at warm temperatures and the reason water holds lots of heat. Hydrogen bonds are also the reason water molecules are attracted to each other and organic material. Without hydrogen bonds, there can be no life."

"I read his book when I was in college. His heavy water process is quite a breakthrough."

"He's going to save the humans."

Aqua sits back in the chair, still puzzled by the news report about the crack under the lake.

Fifteen minutes later, the door to Dr. Bond's office opens. Crystal Penguin walks out.

"Good morning," Crystal says to Aqua. "How are you?"

"Busy."

"Isn't everyone. You wouldn't believe the amount of money the television networks are paying for the celebration. I can't count all the zeros."

Aqua just looks at her.

"Are you meeting with Dr. Bond?" Crystal asks.

"Yes."

"I hope you are prepared. His attention to detail is amazing. He's the smartest penguin in the world. He's smarter than any human too, and I've met heads of states, captains of industry, and billionaires. If you'll excuse me, I have a tour to host."

A half-hour later, Jewel's phone rings. "Aqua, Dr. Bond will see you now."

Aqua gathers her material and opens one of the large ice doors to Dr. Bond's office. She is blinded by light. Thirty feet across the office is a large window overlooking the lake, through which the morning sun is shining.

Pillars stand on either side of the window, reaching from the floor to the ceiling. Dr. Bond stands behind his enormous ice desk, gazing out the window onto his masterpiece. His dark body is but a small silhouette around which the sun blazes into the room and reflects off his ice desk.

The walls are filled with pictures of Dr. Bond with famous humans and magazine covers featuring his smiling face. The words "Perfect Synergistic Strategy" are printed on several magazine covers. A bookcase displays college diplomas, awards, and dozens of books, including several copies of the books he wrote.

But Aqua's attention is focused on Celsius, sitting at Dr. Bond's large guest table with his fins crossed tightly in front of his chest.

"Come in," Dr. Bond says cordially. He walks over to Aqua. "I'm Dr. Bond, Dr. Hydrogen Bond. I've heard good things about you." Dr. Bond extends his fin.

"I'm Aqua Azure Penguin. It's a pleasure to meet you." Aqua touches the underside of his fin with hers, a formal gesture of respect.

"Celsius told me about your accident with the yacht," Dr. Bond says. "Fortunately, it wasn't serious. Please have a seat."

IMAGINE SOLVING THE MOST COMPLEX PROBLEMS

"I knew Celsius would blame me," Aqua says to herself.

Nitro enters.

"You know Nitro," Celsius says to Dr. Bond. "I asked him to join us."

"Of course," Dr. Bond says, walking over to Nitro. "Congratulations on your promotion." Dr. Bond and Nitro slap fins, a gesture of friendship.

Dr. Bond sits closest to the screen, next to Celsius. Nitro sits on the other side of Celsius. Aqua sits on the other side of the table by herself.

Aqua swallows a lump in her throat. She tells herself to exhale. She did not expect Celsius, much less Nitro.

Dr. Bond smiles. "I've got fifteen minutes, and then I'm meeting with an important customer. I understand you want to talk about a crack under our lake."

"Yes," Aqua says, her voice cracking. She quickly lays out large pictures, showing the size of the crack at weekly intervals. Each picture has a date and dimensions of the crack.

"These pictures show the crack has grown from 100 feet long four weeks ago to 2,000 feet long as of yesterday."

Dr. Bond stands and looks at the pictures. Celsius and Nitro also stand. Dr. Bond nods his head affirmatively.

"We aren't lucky enough that the penguin in the pictures is shrinking?" Celsius jokes.

"That's Frostbite," Aqua says. "He's one of our engineers."

"Very good," Dr. Bond says. "What else do you have?" He glances at his watch.

"Frostbite and I measured the tensile strength of the ice at the bottom of the lake in several places. The ice directly over the crack is very weak. It practically falls apart. I brought a sample. We had to tunnel through forty-five feet of slush to get it." She stands, picks up the cooler, and places it on the table.

Dr. Bonds gives a disapproving glance. Aqua quickly puts the cooler back on the floor.

Aqua continues: "The granular size of the ice on the lake bottom directly over the crack is very large and soaked with water. As you know the larger the granular size, the weaker the ice."

She places pictures of ice on the table in front of Dr. Bond. "Sir, the data show the crack is caused by weak ice under the south side of the lake being unable to support the weight of the lake. I strongly recommend we drain a significant portion of the lake to remove stress." She pauses, and then adds, "Immediately."

"Thank you for your concern, but draining the lake won't be necessary," Dr. Bond says reassuringly.

"But sir, the lake is now nearly forty billion gallons. It's 60 percent bigger than planned, and we have a large crack growing right underneath very weak ice. I talked to the Purchasing Department, and we can drain ten billion gallons by Sunday."

"Thank you. Please sit." Aqua sits down.

Dr. Bond sighs. "I wish I had time to teach iceberg science to the employees."

Dr. Bond glances at his watch. "Let me show you the scientific facts about this iceberg. Then you will understand why this iceberg will support very large lakes for many years. Nitro, you were there." Dr. Bond looks at Nitro. Nitro smiles and nods.

Dr. Bond turns on his sleek tablet computer and opens

IMAGINE SOLVING THE MOST COMPLEX PROBLEMS

a program. "I created this program to model the strength of icebergs when I was completing my PhD. The key is the amount of solid ice, not snow-packed ice. Let me find the Atlantis. Here it is."

A colorful image appears; bright white on the top, transitioning to light blue, and then dark blue on the bottom.

Dr. Bond continues: "This image is based upon multiple X-rays. The dark blue is solid ice. Solid ice is formed when pressure exerted by the weight of the snow causes the snow to melt and then refreeze into solid ice. The white on top is snowpack. Here's where the lake is. As you can see, there are 500 feet of solid ice under the lake, which, of course, is all under water. The crack that you found is a normal consequence of underwater melting. Did you investigate underside cracks that are not under the lake?"

"Yes, and I did not see any cracks of any size."

"I'd suggest you look again. I'm quite sure you will find cracks due to melting there as well."

Dr. Bond looks at Celsius. "Between now and the end of the celebration, I do not want any tankers here. Is that clear?"

"Yes sir." Celsius nods.

"I am providing certain networks with coverage of our last-minute preparations, and they are paying a king's ransom for it, actually several kings' ransoms."

Dr. Bond breaks into a boyish grin that quickly turns stern. "But I do worry about the banks of the lake because the lake is much larger than planned. I do not want any leaks. Celsius, please make sure the banks are secure."

"I'll take care of it." Celsius nods.

ICEBERG DOWN: BUILDING HIGH-PERFORMANCE TEAMS

Dr. Bond looks directly at Celsius, then Nitro, and then Aqua. "Let us not forget that we are accomplishing the greatest feat in penguin history. Failure is not an option."

Celsius and Nitro smile and nod.

"Now, if you'll excuse me, I have an important meeting."

Dr. Bond walks behind his desk and searches through some folders.

Celsius looks at Aqua and shakes his head as if to say, *"You idiot."* He and Nitro leave while Aqua packs up her material. Aqua leaves.

"This is silly," Aqua says to herself. She turns and reenters Dr. Bond's office.

"Dr. Bond."

"Yes," he says without looking up.

"Your X-rays are three years old. They were taken before there was a lake on the iceberg. Could we take another set of X-rays of the ice under the lake to make sure the ice is still solid?"

"That won't be necessary," Dr. Bond says, still searching for something on his disorganized desk.

"You know water seeping into the cracks in ice reduces the tensile strength of the ice. We have no way of knowing how strong the ice is under the lake right now. All we know is the crack is growing. We can't ignore this data. I really think we should drain the lake to a safe …"

"No!" Dr. Bond's eyes narrow as he meets Aqua's gaze. "Now, if you'll excuse me, I have an important meeting."

Chapter 12

Someone Has to be Blamed

Disappointed, Aqua carries her presentation back to the maintenance office. She opens the cooler. The ice from under the south side of the lake has broken apart.

Her cell phone rings. It's Celsius' assistant. She tells Aqua to report to Celsius' office immediately.

Aqua's heart rate quickens the closer she gets to Celsius' office. She enters and is surprised to find both Celsius and Crystal. Celsius' face is red.

"Sit down," Celsius says, pointing to a chair at his guest table. Aqua sits. Celsius walks toward Aqua, and stands directly in front of her. Crystal turns her back to Aqua.

"Did you tell the media we have a crack under the lake?" Celsius asks.

"Absolutely not," Aqua replies.

Crystal turns and says, "Did you tell anyone who is not an employee of Atlantis?"

"No, I didn't." Aqua pauses and remembers she asked

Aristotle for advice. "I did mention it to someone I knew in college, but I'm sure he kept it to himself."

"I knew it," Celsius exclaims.

"What is his name?" Chrystal asks.

"I've known him for years. He wouldn't …"

"What is his name?!" Celsius demands.

"Aristotle Penguin," Aqua says softly.

"Aristotle Penguin!" Crystal exclaims. "He's the CEO of Glacier Fresh Water. He's a competitor. He's using it against us!"

"He wouldn't …"

"He just did!" Celsius thunders. Celsius points his fin at Aqua. "You have committed a serious breach of confidentiality. You will receive a written reprimand."

"I have to tell Dr. Bond," Crystal says, pursing her lips and shaking her head. "I will not let Atlantis be disparaged by a third-rate competitor." Crystal leaves.

Aqua stands to leave.

"Sit down!" Celsius yells. Aqua sits. Celsius circles Aqua like a shark. "You know what your problem is? You simply don't do what you're asked."

Celsius paces back and forth. After a few seconds, he stops and glares at Aqua. "You and me, we joined Atlantis around the same time. Since then, I've been promoted twice while you have remained in the same job. If that is cause for resentment, you need to get over it. If I catch you going behind my back again, you will be fired. Is that clear?"

Aqua nods.

"You're excused."

Chapter 13

Iceberg Down

Monday Morning 7:45

"Come on, Frostbite," Aqua yells back into the maintenance office. "The storm has finally stopped. Let's see how big the lake is. Can you believe this fog?"

"Come look at this!" Frostbite calls.

Aqua enters the maintenance office. The Penguin News channel is showing live video of the stunning beauty of the Atlantis Iceberg shrouded in a bright white cloud. The announcer says, "Atlantis looks like it's from another world. It's heavenly."

"The iceberg is cooling the humid air," Aqua says. "Water vapor has condensed into a cloud around the iceberg."

Frostbite shuffles through supplies on his desk. "I found my calculator. I want to calculate how much water is in the lake. We received more than five inches of rain."

"Come on," Aqua calls. "Let's get to the lake before the media circus begins."

"Aqua," Frostbite yells from behind. "How did your meeting go with Dr. Bond?"

"Some days you have to come to work prepared to be fired."

"What?!"

"Never mind," Aqua says, walking faster.

Aqua and Frostbite arrive at the lake and look at the lake-level measuring stick. Frostbite punches one number into his calculator. "Thirty-nine billion, seven hundred and sixty-two million gallons.

"How did you determine the size of the lake with one number?"

"I wrote a program that calculates the number of gallons." He pauses. "That's odd. There was more water in the lake Friday."

"Are you sure your formula is right?"

"Actually, I'm sure it's wrong," Frostbite jokes. "Formulae are only approximations. What I do know is the lake level was higher Friday than it is today."

"Maybe the banks eroded during the storm, and water spilled into the ocean. It was very windy. Waves from the lake could have breached the banks. Let's walk around the lake and check for evidence of spilling."

They walk quickly around the lake. By the time they return, the fog has lifted, and the sun glistens off the wet ice.

"No evidence of water spilling over the banks," Frostbite says.

"The media circus has begun," Aqua points to dozens of yachts and cruise ships dropping anchor at the new docks on the south side of the iceberg. Humans are climbing up onto the iceberg with the assistance of penguins. A few dozen humans are already milling around near the lake and statues.

"Here come the TV helicopters," Aqua adds, looking up.

"Wait a minute", Frostbite says looking at the lake-level measuring stick. "Am I hallucinating, or is the lake lower than it was an hour ago? It should be rising. Water from the storm is still entering the lake."

Aqua's face turns pale as the worst-case scenario creeps into her mind. "Oh no! Maybe water is leaking down through the crack under the lake and into the ocean. Let's get our oxygen." Aqua runs back to the maintenance office. Frostbite follows.

Aqua yells, "We forget that the lake and the architecture all depend upon the structural integrity of the iceberg, and 90 percent of it is underwater."

In the maintenance office, Aqua puts on her oxygen tanks. She helps Frostbite on with his.

"Follow me," Aqua shouts. They run a half-mile and jump onto the slide. Soon they are under the iceberg. Aqua swims as fast as she can toward the crack under the lake.

She arrives at the crack, shocked to find it's much larger than it was the last time she checked. She swims up into the crevice. Slowly, she swims from one end toward the other. Frostbite joins her about halfway.

Aqua stops. She feels a strong current of water. She puts her mouth up against the current. It's fresh water. Frostbite does the same and then swims to one side.

Suddenly, a piece of ice the size of a car shoots out of the crack, barely missing Frostbite. The force of the current increases dramatically.

A vision of millions of tons of water filled with ice

crashing down on her and Frostbite flashes through Aqua's mind. *We could be pulverized!*

Aqua motions for Frostbite to swim away from the crack and out from under the iceberg. In thirty minutes of the fastest swimming of their lives, they reach the stairs that will take them back up to the top.

Frostbite sits on the steps to catch his breath. But Aqua knows they are not out of danger yet.

"Get onto the topside and away from the lake!" she yells." They drop their oxygen tanks and climb the rest of the stairs to the top.

Television cameras are everywhere. Shadows from TV helicopters dance on the ice. Extravagant yachts, cruise ships, and sail boats surround the iceberg. Dr. Bond addresses hundreds of the most famous and prestigious humans and penguins in the world. Aqua runs toward the podium. She has to tell someone water is leaking through the crack.

Aqua sees Crystal talking to a group of reporters. She waves at Crystal. Chrystal ignores her. Aqua looks out at the lake. Fortunately all the yachts are tied to the pier.

Aqua runs toward the podium. Celsius and the other executives are standing behind Dr. Bond as cameras click furiously.

Aqua runs toward Celsius. "Iceberg Down," she yells. He can't hear her.

A familiar human approaches the podium. It's the Secretary-General of the United Nations. "Dr. Bond. It is my great pleasure to announce that you are this year's recipient of the United Nations Humanitarian Award. Congratulations."

Aqua looks again at Crystal. She is cheering. Aqua runs

back over to Crystal.

"Crystal, Iceberg Down," Aqua says, panting. "Water from the lake is gushing through the crack into the …"

"Not now!" Crystal says angrily and walks away.

"You can't ignore Iceberg Down!" Aqua yells.

Under Aqua's feet, a slight trembling begins. One by one, humans and penguins look around. The trembling becomes louder. The Secretary-General stops talking. Cameras stop taking pictures. Everyone is frozen in place.

Baboom!! The iceberg suddenly drops twenty feet straight down. Humans and penguins sprawl across the ice. Castles collapse. Statues fall.

Aqua pulls herself to her feet as the iceberg slowly rocks back up and then down again. A twenty-foot-tall tsunami wave rises up from the lake and rolls across the ice. Humans scream as the water knocks them down and drags them into the ice cold lake.

Aqua and other penguins dive into the lake. Fighting waves and strong currents, the penguins push the panic-stricken humans to shore. Other penguins arrive with blankets. Paramedics attend to the freezing and frightened humans. Soon, all the humans are safe and onshore.

Helicopters swoop in for close-up videos as the two giant pieces of the iceberg move slowly apart.

An hour later, the fresh water lake has completely disappeared.

Tears run down Aqua's face. She knew this could have been prevented if only her superiors had taken her warnings seriously.

Part I Summary

Until the iceberg broke, Dr. Bond was hailed as a great leader; a visionary who didn't take no for an answer. He was a world-renowned expert. He created an action-oriented culture that did not tolerate problems, mistakes, or excuses. He was always positive. He had a laser-like focus on customers. These are qualities typically used to describe a strong leader.

Dr. Bond faced two complex problems: how to extract water from icebergs and how to make more profit than he could make selling water alone.

Dr. Bond came up with two innovative solutions. To harvest water from icebergs, he melted the top of an iceberg and created a large lake. To make more money, he built a resort that featured the lake as its main attraction.

Dr. Bond called it the perfect synergistic strategy. Without the lake, there would be little interest in the resort. Without the resort, there would be little return on investment. Experts like Colonel Tierney hailed Dr. Bond's strategy as brilliant.

The resort made so much money that Dr. Bond decided to build ten more lakes on ten more icebergs, all with resorts.

As a grand finale before draining the lake, Dr. Bond planned a giant celebration, which required that draining the lake be delayed yet again.

But one of his employees, Aqua Penguin, discovered a crack under the iceberg directly under the lake. She was worried that water from the lake was seeping into the ice and weakening the ice, and that the weight of the giant lake was applying the force creating the crack. She gathered data and presented it to her boss, Celsius.

After approaching Celsius several times, Aqua scheduled a meeting with Dr. Bond. To Aqua's surprise, Dr. Bond invited Celsius, and Celsius invited Nitro.

The meeting with Dr. Bond was a smile-and-nod meeting. In a smile-and-nod meeting, the leader patronizes the attendees and controls the outcome. Everyone else in the meeting is supposed to smile-and-nod, to indicate their agreement with everything the leader says.[2]

Celsius and Nitro behaved as Dr. Bond wanted. They smiled and nodded on cue.

Aqua, however, did not smile or nod, even after Dr. Bond politely told her draining the lake would not be necessary. Instead, Aqua continued to press her opinion that the lake should be drained to a safe level. Finally, Dr. Bond yelled, "No."

Dr. Bond achieved the outcome he desired. The lake was not drained.

Aqua failed to persuade Dr. Bond to drain the lake. Worse, despite working hard to prevent accidents, she was blamed for the minor accident with the yacht. Aqua was also blamed for leaking the news about the crack under the lake to the media.

The story points out two detrimental consequences of smile-and-nod meetings.
1. Issues and dissenting ideas are suppressed, which can reduce organizational performance and cause failure.
2. Job security and career advancement can depend more upon smiling and nodding in meetings than job performance.

The weekend before the celebration, a storm hit the iceberg. Then, during the celebration, the iceberg broke. All the fresh water spilled into the ocean. Not a single drop was delivered to customers.

With Atlantis failing to provide water to humans, the water emergency worsened. Is there another approach? Will it work in time to save the humans?

Part II: Learning to Succeed

Chapter 14

The Road Back

A Month Later

Aqua hears a knock at her door. She hasn't had many visitors at her small apartment in Penguin City. She opens the door to find Frostbite, dripping wet and panting.

"Frostbite, it's good to see you. What are you doing here?"

"I swam here from the Lagoon. I made it in less than three hours. I could use a glass of water, the saltier the better."

Aqua pours Frostbite a large glass of salty water.

Frostbite guzzles it and takes a deep breath. "That's better. I'm working at Glacier Fresh Water next to the Lagoon below Renaissance Village. The company wants to enter the iceberg business."

"Can you back up a little and tell me what you've been doing the past month?"

"After the disaster, I went home. It's a small town a hundred miles west of here. Every time I turned on the

TV, I had to watch another video of the iceberg breaking, humans screaming, and commentators describing the event as the worst disaster in penguin history. Then, the endless interviews with Dr. Know-It-All blaming the storm. In one interview, he even said his workforce should have been better trained. Can you believe he blames us?"

"Yes! I can't stand to look at him. I don't watch TV. I don't read newspapers. I don't go online. I live like a hermit – me and my photography."

"I'm sorry to hear that. I decided I had to find another job. I posted my resume online, and Glacier Fresh Water called me. I started a week ago. They're nothing like Atlantis."

"I'm going back to school this fall and finishing my degree, finally."

"That's great. I talked to the CEO of Glacier Fresh Water, Aristotle Penguin. He said he knows you, and he wants to talk to you."

"We had a few classes together at Penguin University. He was definitely an out-of-the-box thinker. He and his wife ran the Age of Enlightenment Theater."

"Now his wife runs the theater. He runs Glacier Fresh Water. I'm staying in his guest house until I find an apartment. He asked me to give you this." Frostbite hands Aqua an envelope in a waterproof bag.

"Thanks. How can I reach you?"

"Here's my business card. I love Renaissance Village. Last night, I went to the Age of Enlightenment Theater to listen to some great jazz music."

"I was born there."

"I'm never leaving." Frostbite glances at his waterproof watch. "I've got to get back. Tomorrow's a work day."

IMAGINE SOLVING THE MOST COMPLEX PROBLEMS

Frostbite opens the door to leave. "Call Aristotle."

"I'll think about it."

Aqua opens the envelope and finds a note folded around a picture of her, Aristotle, and two other classmates. The note reads: "I ran across this picture. Hope to see you soon." It is signed, "With warm affection, Aristotle". A phone number is written on the bottom.

Aqua gazes at the picture. *"It can't hurt to talk to Aristotle,"* she thinks. *"Besides, I want to know if he leaked the news about the crack under the lake to the media."*

Aqua calls Aristotle and reaches his receptionist. She makes an appointment for the next day.

Chapter 15

Too Good to Be True?

Aqua rises early and swims leisurely to the Lagoon, stopping along the way to explore the underwater mysteries and take pictures. She can't stop thinking about what happened at Atlantis. She is determined to never again work for someone who doesn't trust her.

Aqua arrives at the Lagoon and hops ashore. She walks up to the factory. It's a large greenhouse built around a glacier, just before the tongue of the glacier enters the lagoon. She arrives in the lobby ten minutes early. It's small but elegant, with a shelf of ice trophies. It's nothing like the pretentiousness of Atlantis, but no less beautiful.

"Are you Aqua Azure Penguin?" the receptionist asks.

"Yes, I am," Aqua nods.

"I'm Sauna Aquifer Penguin. It's very nice to meet you. Aristotle's office is right through that door. He is looking forward to seeing you. Please let yourself in."

Aqua walks to his office. The door is open, but she

IMAGINE SOLVING THE MOST COMPLEX PROBLEMS

knocks lightly.

"Come in." Aristotle smiles, as he stands behind his desk and ambles over to Aqua. He extends his fin. She touches the underside of his fin respectfully. Aristotle slaps her fin gently.

"Have a seat." Aqua and Aristotle sit in chairs across from each other. "Can I offer you a drink?"

"No, thank you."

"I'm sorry about Atlantis. You were right about the crack under the lake."

"Yes, I was right. The media found out about the crack under the lake. Did you tell anyone?"

Aristotle's smile vanishes. "No, I didn't tell anyone."

Aqua looks at him for a moment, bewildered. "At this point, it's water under the bridge, or should I say water under the iceberg. I'd like to hear about your company."

"Well, let's see… I took out a loan against the Age of Enlightenment Theater and started the Glacier Fresh Water Company. We've been melting this glacier with a greenhouse for five years, and we're getting better at it all the time. Guess what the hardest part is?"

"I'd say the hardest part is scheduling tankers so they are here when the holding pond has water."

"You're right. Melting depends upon the weather, and the weather is unpredictable. We found ourselves in situations where we either had a tanker and no water, or water and no tanker. When we had water and no tanker, we'd scramble to dig holes to store water. If the tanker didn't arrive soon enough, the water would freeze. Most important, digging holes distracted us from our primary responsibility, which is melting efficiency. How do you think we solved the problem?"

"Bigger holding pond?"

"We did the opposite. We decided to stop melting the glacier if the holding pond was full. We control melting by opening and closing windows and curtains. Initially, we had to stop melting almost every day. In the last two months we didn't stop once. Then we started finding ways to increase efficiency. Before we knew it, efficiency had doubled."

"Frostbite mentioned you want to enter the iceberg business."

"Yes. Each year enough new icebergs form in Antarctica to meet one-third of the freshwater needs for the entire human population and all human industries. I want to figure out how to capture some of the fresh water and provide to it humans. I'm always looking for employees who can bring good ideas to the table."

"I want to be honest with you. I'm planning to go back to college this fall and finish my degree."

"You can finish your degree while working here. We have several penguins taking online courses from Penguin University. We also have a tutor program where employees volunteer to tutor students. I teach a course on how to tutor. The tutor training course also serves as preparation for anyone interested in management."

"That sounds like a wonderful opportunity."

"We run a skeleton shift in the winter for special projects, like iceberg investigation. In the spring, we bring everyone back to work. I asked a few penguins to come in today to talk to you. Do you have any questions?"

"No, but I imagine I'll have some later."

"Follow me," Aristotle says.

Three hours later, Aqua returns to Aristotle's office.

IMAGINE SOLVING THE MOST COMPLEX PROBLEMS

"What do you think?" Aristotle asks her.

"Impressive. I have a question. Everyone talks of openness and admitting mistakes and raising issues without fear. Do you find penguins are reluctant to do that?"

"Good question. Let me first explain my philosophy. We live in a complex and uncertain world. Relying upon the boss or an expert to make the tough decisions doesn't work anymore. In fact, catastrophe often results. Atlantis is a perfect example: Dr. Bond tried to solve a complex problem. His solution was very innovative, but it didn't work because the lake injected stress into the iceberg that helped cause failure. Customers were not satisfied. Investors lost their money, and employees felt a sense of failure. The more complex the problem, the harder it is to achieve both innovation and quality."

"Why is that?"

"Because quality is achieved by removing variation, and innovation introduces variation, which can cause failure."

"How do you achieve both quality and innovation in today's complex and uncertain world?"

"That's the second part of my philosophy: I believe we can find innovative solutions to the most complex problems and achieve very high quality if we work together effectively. Doing so requires that we learn from experiences, particularly failures, which means raising issues, admitting mistakes, and making problems visible."

"I'm sorry, but that's not the way the world works. Nobody gets ahead by admitting mistakes, and nobody wants his problems shown off to the whole organization."

Aristotle smiles. "That's because most managers are in denial. Managers tell employees that problems and mistakes shouldn't happen and won't be tolerated. All the evidence is to the contrary. Problems are out there, and everyone makes mistakes. If the goal is innovation, new and different problems are going to be created, and new and different mistakes are going to be made. Pretending otherwise pretty much ensures complex problems will not be solved."

"It makes more sense than blaming each other."

"Would you like to join us?"

Aqua didn't expect an offer so soon. "Are you offering me a job on the glacier side of the business or on icebergs?"

"As I mentioned, we won't resume fresh water production from the glacier until spring. Right now I'm looking for penguins with experience in icebergs."

Aqua draws a deep breath. "I accept." She smiles. "Can I start a week from Monday?"

"Absolutely." Aristotle stands and extends his fin, which Aqua slaps softly. "Please stop by Sauna's desk and pick up an application. We need an application for your employee file."

Aqua walks over to Sauna's desk, and tells her she has accepted a job and will start a week from Monday.

"Wonderful." Sauna retrieves a file folder from her desk drawer. "You're the fourth one from Atlantis. Do you know Celsius and Nitro? They're starting this coming Monday."

Aqua's jaw drops. "Did you say Celsius and Nitro work here?"

"Yes, do you know them?"

Aqua turns and walks straight for the door.

"Your application."

Aqua marches outside. She's hyper-ventilating. She

IMAGINE SOLVING THE MOST COMPLEX PROBLEMS

paces back and forth. She dives into the lagoon and sprints into the ocean. She stops and takes a deep breath.

It's okay. I'll just tell Aristotle I've reconsidered.

Aqua swims back, hops ashore, and reenters the building.

"Are you all right?" Sauna asks.

"Yes, thank you. Is Aristotle in?"

"Yes."

The door to Aristotle's office is still open. He is placing a folder into his briefcase. She knocks on the door.

"Come in, Aqua. What can I do for you?"

"I've reconsidered. I will not be joining your company."

"Please, have a seat." Aristotle sets down his briefcase.

"I don't want to take up your time." Aqua remains in the doorway.

"Would you mind telling me what changed your mind?"

"I'm not interested in working on icebergs again. I'd rather focus on finishing my degree. Thanks anyway." She turns to leave.

"Are there penguins working here that you do not want to work with?"

Sauna told him.

Aqua stands silent in the doorway.

"Please, have a seat."

Aqua shrugs her shoulder and sits down. She crosses her fins tightly in front of her.

"Do you think the failure at Atlantis was caused by bad penguins or a bad system?" Aristotle asks.

Aqua jumps up. "I really have to be going."

"Please. This is important."

"Okay." Aqua taps her foot. "Explain what caused Atlantis to fail."

Aristotle's speaks softly. "What happened at Atlantis is normal given the complexity of the situation."

"Are you kidding me?" Aqua blurts out.

"Actually, I'm not. Behavior in complex situations has been studied at length. We know that in complex situations, we tend to jump to conclusions and seek confirmation, not dissention."

"That clears it up for me," Aqua says sarcastically. "Now I'll be on my way."

Aristotle continues: "The reason I'm hiring penguins with experience at Atlantis is so we can collaboratively figure out what went wrong. Then, hopefully, we can figure out how to prevent failures from happening again. Without the first part, we're not likely to achieve the second part."

"You've hired the experts. You don't need me."

"You have a different perspective. You bring different ideas. When tackling complex problems, diversity of ideas is essential."

"I'll save you some time. You want to know why Atlantis failed. It failed because management was a bunch of greedy egomaniacs who punished the individuals who were trying to prevent failure instead of listening. Then guess what? The iceberg broke, just as I predicted. Now the CEO says his workforce needed more training. He and his wild-guessing group of suck-ups are the reason that iceberg broke. So excuse me if I don't want to work with the same buffoons again."

"You believe it's unfair that Dr. Bond blamed the employees. But is it fair to blame him? What if Dr. Bond was caught up in a system where short-term profit

IMAGINE SOLVING THE MOST COMPLEX PROBLEMS

dominated? What if we live in a world that is so complex and uncertain that we either work together or we fail, and failure is often catastrophic? Should we blame the penguins whose decision making was no match for the complexity of the problem, or should we try to fix the system?"

"I'm sorry. What does any of this have to do with me?"

"Are you sure you would have acted differently?"

"All they had to do was drain the lake!" she shouts. Aqua composes herself and adds, "As I suggested many times." She turns and walks away.

Aristotle jumps up from behind his desk and follows her.

"I will pay you a month's salary if you participate in a half-day meeting with your former colleagues this coming Monday."

Aqua stops in her tracks and turns to face him. "A month's salary for a half-day of work?"

"Yes. If you want to join our company after the meeting, fine; if not, I'll hand you a check and you can be on your way. But you have to contribute. I want you to say what's on your mind, and most important, I want you to try to understand why your former colleagues behaved the way they did. You have to try to walk in their shoes."

Aqua looks down for a moment. "Okay. I'll do it."

Chapter 16

Learning to Succeed

The Following Monday

Aqua fidgets in her chair in the lobby. She dreads the idea of spending a half-day with Celsius and Nitro.

"Good morning, Aqua," Sauna says, returning to her desk. "I'm sorry to keep you waiting. Aristotle will be here in a moment. The others are in the large conference room down the hall on the left." She gestures.

Aqua enters the conference room tentatively. *This may be a large conference room here, but it would be a small one at Atlantis.* The conference table seats eight; three on each side and one on each end. Frostbite is on one side of the table. Celsius and Nitro are on the other side, with Celsius in the middle chair.

"Good morning," Aqua says softly.

"Aqua," Frostbite says. "I expected to see you in the guesthouse." He slaps her fin.

"I woke up early and swam in this morning. Aqua sits next to Frostbite, directly across from Celsius.

IMAGINE SOLVING THE MOST COMPLEX PROBLEMS

"Good morning," Aqua says to Celsius and Nitro.

"Aristotle told me you joined his company," Celsius says. "Then he told me you didn't."

"That is correct. I am just here today."

Celsius continues to look at Aqua, expecting her to elaborate. She looks away.

Aristotle enters the room. "Good morning everyone. I call what we will do today 'Learning-to-Succeed.' As I've told you all, I'm interested in figuring out how we can safely and reliably extract fresh water from icebergs. The first step is learning why Atlantis failed. We are not here to blame anyone, but I do want to understand what happened. I've discussed Atlantis with each of you, and you each bring a different perspective. I expect there will be disagreements. Please remember, disagreements are opportunities to learn."

Aristotle walks to the front of the room. "Before we start, I would like each of you to tell when you joined Atlantis and why. Who wants to go first?"

"I'll go," Celsius says. "Dr. Bond was famous, and he was the champion of a noble cause. I saw him on TV giving speeches. I read about him everywhere. His company needed licensed architects and managers. I have an undergraduate degree in architecture and a master's degree in business administration. Dr. Bond hired me a year ago." He pauses. "I was so in love with the architecture, I couldn't wait to get to work each morning."

Nitro clears his throat. "I was the first employee Dr. Bond hired. Atlantis needed explosives and carving experts, and I had extensive experience. I started three years ago. What we created on the top of that iceberg was a miracle."

Aqua rolls her eyes.

"Aqua, Frostbite?" Aristotle says.

"I joined Atlantis a year ago to provide fresh water to humans," Aqua says quickly.

"I joined for the same reason," Frostbite says, "two months before the iceberg broke."

"Aqua, what did you think about the architecture?"

"As I said, I joined Atlantis to provide fresh water to humans. The architecture wasn't important to me."

"Frostbite, is there anything you want to add?"

"The architecture was impressive, but it didn't help us provide water to humans."

Thank you," Aristotle says. "I'd like you each to prepare a Five-Why diagram. Five-Why is a deductive reasoning root-cause analysis tool. The goal is to find the root causes, which when altered, solve the problem. The actual root causes are often hidden behind other causes. Too often these intermediate causes are altered, which may relieve the problem for a while but won't prevent its recurrence. Here is an example."

Problem: Production machine stopped operating.

1. Why did the machine stop?
   →Because there was an overload and the fuse blew.
2. Why was there an overload?
   →Because the bearing was not lubricated adequately.
3. Why was the bearing not lubricated adequately?
   →Because the lubrication pump was not pumping properly.
4. Why wasn't the lubrication pump pumping properly?
   →Because the shaft of the pump was worn.
5. Why was the pump shaft worn?
   →Because the strainer was not attached, and metal scrap got into it.[3]

IMAGINE SOLVING THE MOST COMPLEX PROBLEMS

Aristotle checks his notes. "The first question is: why did the problem occur. In each iteration the problem solver asks why the previous condition occurred until the root causes are revealed. For example, if the problem solver doesn't probe deeply enough to find that the strainer was not attached, he might replace the fuse or the pump shaft. Worse, he might write a maintenance procedure instructing workers to check and replace the fuse or pump shaft every time the machine stops. Doing so could result in unnecessary expense and machine downtime. Any questions?"

Everyone is silent.

"Our first question is, 'Why did Atlantis fail to provide water to humans?' After you answer that question, ask why the answer happened. Continue until you find the root causes. We have plenty of flip-chart paper. When you're done, attach your Five-Why diagram to the wall. We'll discuss your responses, and combine them later. Bear in mind that I will ask what evidence you have that supports your conclusions."

"Can I work with Celsius?" Nitro asks.

"You may if you want, but you will get more out of the exercise if you work alone."

Aqua leans back in her chair and closes her eyes; so many images flood her mind as she recalls the conversations and events leading up to the iceberg disaster.

When she looks up, she sees Celsius and Nitro attaching their Five-Why diagram to the wall. *They're blaming it on a perfect storm. They're merely repeating Dr. Bond's sound-bites from his interviews. It's about time somebody tells the truth. Besides, I don't have to suck up to anybody. I don't work here.*

A few minutes later, Aristotle asks, "Are we done?"

Everyone nods affirmatively.

"Who wants to go first?"

"We will," Celsius says as he stands next to his Five-Why diagram. "Atlantis failed because the iceberg broke. The iceberg broke because of a perfect storm of unforeseeable events in the form of a giant storm one week before we planned to drain the lake."

Celsius, Nitro Five-Why

1. Why did Atlantis fail to provide water to humans?
   →Because the iceberg broke.
2. Why did the iceberg break?
   →Because of a perfect storm of unforeseeable events (e.g., giant storm hit one week before the lake was to be drained).

"I'm curious about the storm," Aristotle says. "How bad was it?"

"We had over five inches of rain, lots of wind, and very big waves."

"Is that abnormal?"

"Yes. What are the chances of a storm like that hitting one week before we planned to drain the lake?"

"I did some research," Aristotle says. "In the last decade, Melbourne has had seventeen storms of that magnitude or worse."

"Are you saying a perfect storm is not the root cause?"

"It may be a root cause, but it's probably not the only root cause. Let's see what the others have."

Frostbite looks at Aqua.

"You go," Aqua says.

Frostbite takes a deep breath. "Atlantis failed to provide water to humans because the iceberg broke. The iceberg broke because it was unable to withstand the stress, part of which was from the storm, and part was from the weight of the lake. One reason the iceberg was unable to withstand the stress is because water from the lake seeped into the ice and weakened it."

<u>Frostbite Five-Why</u>

1. Why did Atlantis fail to provide water to humans?
   →Because the iceberg broke.
2. Why did the iceberg break?
   →Because the iceberg was unable to withstand the stress (storm, weight of the lake, etc.).
3. Why was the iceberg unable to withstand the stress?
   →One reason is water from the lake seeped into the ice and weakened it.

"How do you know water from the lake weakened the iceberg?" Celsius asks.

"We collected lots of evidence, but the most concrete evidence was when Aqua and I were under the iceberg, shortly before it broke. Fresh water was flowing rapidly out the crack."

"It was?" Celsius says.

"Along with very large pieces of ice," Aqua adds.

"Really?" Celsius says.

"Really," Aqua answers

"Wow," Nitro says.

"Other questions?" Aristotle asks.

After a moment of silence, Aristotle says, "Aqua?"

"I should have mentioned the storm. Anyway, Atlantis failed because the iceberg broke. It broke because water seeped into the ice and weakened it. Water seeped into the ice because the lake was too big. The lake was too big because draining was delayed multiple times. Draining was delayed because management didn't care about the integrity of the ice under the lake. Management didn't care about the integrity of the ice under the lake because profit and fame were higher priority than fresh water for humans and safety of employees and guests."

<u>Aqua Five-Why</u>

1. Why did Atlantis fail to provide water to humans?
   →Because the iceberg broke.
2. Why did the iceberg break?
   →Because water from the lake seeped into the ice and weakened it.
3. Why did water seep into the ice?
   →Because the lake was too big.
4. Why was the lake too big?
   →Because draining the lake was delayed multiple times.
5. Why was draining delayed?
   →Because management didn't care about the integrity of the ice under the lake.
6. Why didn't management care about the ice under the lake?
   →Because profit and fame were higher priority than water for humans and safety of employees and guests.

Aristotle says, "Before we …

Celsius interrupts. "What makes you think management didn't care about the integrity of the ice under the lake?"

"Because I raised the issue of the crack under the lake for weeks. I brought pictures and ice samples. But nobody cared."

"Wait a minute. What you fail to realize is I told Dr. Bond several times there was a crack under the lake. He simply didn't listen."

IMAGINE SOLVING THE MOST COMPLEX PROBLEMS

Aqua quickly writes, "Dr. Bond doesn't listen" on her Five-Why diagram. "Gee, we almost missed that one," she says sarcastically.

"It's hard to have patience with employees who question everything they're asked to do and then go behind your back. It's so much easier working with team players like Nitro who just do what they're asked without complaining!"

"Do you have any idea how close we came to killing humans and penguins?" Aqua writes, "Psychopath" on her Five-Why diagram.

"Nitro, Frostbite," Aristotle says. "Can you excuse us for a moment? I want to get to the bottom of this."

Nitro and Frostbite leave.

"This is a waste of my time," Aqua announces as she stands. "If you'll excuse me, I'll be on my way."

"Can you give me five minutes and then make that decision?"

Aqua sits. "Five minutes!"

"Thank you." Aristotle sits at the head of the table. He speaks softly. "Atlantis experienced a failure of catastrophic proportion. I'm curious. Celsius, where were you when the iceberg broke?"

"I was standing behind Dr. Bond with the other executives. The media were taking pictures non-stop. I couldn't see because of the constant flash from the camera bulbs. Then the explosion knocked me down. I honestly didn't know what had happened. Then I heard the screams. When I could see again, I helped wrap blankets around the wet humans."

"Thank you," Aristotle says. "Aqua, where were you?"

"First thing Monday morning, Frostbite and I noticed

the lake level was slightly lower than it was on Friday, which was odd considering how much rain we had. We walked around the lake looking for leaks in the banks. When we didn't find any, it occurred to me that lake water might be leaking through the crack under the iceberg. We swam under the iceberg and found fresh water gushing through the crack. It was an Iceberg Down condition. When we returned to the top, I ran around yelling Iceberg Down, but everyone was too busy sucking up to the media. Then the iceberg broke."

Celsius says, "If the iceberg had broken a few minutes earlier, you and Frostbite would have been killed."

"We were lucky."

"I'm sorry."

Aristotle says, "I saws videos of humans being rescued from the lake."

"A tsunami rose up and dragged dozens of humans into the lake," Aqua says. "We pulled them out."

"Who's we?" Aristotle asks.

"I was one of the first in. I saw Frostbite and Nitro in the water and many other penguins. I saw Celsius on the shore wrapping humans with blankets."

"You should be proud that you saved the humans. Imagine how much worse it would have been if heads of states had been killed."

"I guess."

"Aqua, why did you go behind Celsius' back and make an appointment with Dr. Bond."

"It appeared Celsius was not keeping Dr. Bond informed about the risk posed by the crack under the lake. I offered to show my pictures to Dr. Bond, but Celsius kept telling me that he would handle it."

"Celsius, did you consider having Aqua present the data directly to Dr. Bond?"

"When I raised the issue with Dr. Bond, he told me the iceberg was very strong and not to worry about it. He also told me he didn't want rumors spreading so close to the celebration."

"Did you follow up as the crack became worse?"

"Yes, and I sent all of Aqua's pictures and data to Dr. Bond."

"I'm curious. Do you know if Dr. Bond actually looked at the pictures and data? Did he ask any questions?"

"He told me not to worry about it. He also reminded me of my other responsibilities. I had just been promoted and had far more to do than time to do it. I did as I was told."

"Is there anything else?"

"Yes, Atlantis was Dr. Bond's company. He made the decisions. He expected us to implement his decisions, not question his decisions."

"Aqua, are you willing to proceed?"

"I guess."

"I'm going to bring Nitro and Frostbite back in now."

They return. Aristotle walks to the wall. "I should have mentioned that a Five-Why exercise should not be used to blame others. Although Aqua may assume things about her colleagues, she isn't in a position to know. Only Celsius can speak for Celsius, and only Dr. Bond can speak for Dr. Bond. Now we're going to combine what we have so far. Do we all agree that Atlantis failed to provide fresh water because the iceberg broke?"

Everyone nods.

"Do we all agree the iceberg broke because it was

unable to withstand the stress?"

"Yes."

"Do we all agree that one reason the iceberg was unable to withstand the stress is because water from the lake seeped into the ice?"

"Yes."

"Do we all agree that water seeped into the ice because the lake was too big, and it was too big because draining was delayed multiple times?"

Frostbite raises his fin. Aristotle nods for him to proceed.

"Although it is true that the storm added stress to the iceberg and water from the lake weakened the ice under the lake, we should not assume these are the only two factors that caused the iceberg to break. Lots of other factors determine the strength of an iceberg and the stress it is under."

"We've come as far as a Five-Why analysis will take us," Aristotle says. "Frostbite's Five-Why diagram sums it up."

"What about leadership?" Aqua says. "Leadership is the reason Atlantis failed."

"We'll get to leadership. Next, I want to create a cause-and-effect timeline showing the sequence of events that led to Atlantis' failure. Nitro, you were there from the beginning. Can you tell us what happened?"

"Right after I was hired, I helped Dr. Bond X-ray icebergs. Dr. Bond selected the first one we X-rayed."

"Then what happened?"

"After choosing the iceberg, Dr. Bond approached banks for a loan. Then he met Colonel Tierney. Colonel Tierney wanted to make money while we were filling the lake, so Dr. Bond decided to build a resort. After securing financing from Colonel Tierney, whales pushed the iceberg from the Ross Ice Shelf to Melbourne. We hired penguins and started digging the hole for the lake and the canals to feed the lake. Then we started building the resort. It took eighteen months, basically two summers, to fill the lake."

Aristotle looks puzzled. "Are you saying Atlantis had water to provide humans for a year-and-a-half and never delivered any?"

"Yes. Dr. Bond's goal was to create a lake with 25 billion gallons of fresh water. We reached nearly 40 billion gallons before the iceberg broke."

"Thank you. The first decision was selecting an iceberg on which to build a lake of fresh water. The second decision was building a resort. A lot of time was spent implementing those decisions. What were the results?"

Nitro answers. "We quickly had fresh water in the lake that could have been sold. Then the resort started making lots of money. That was the big surprise. The resort made far more money than could be made selling water. Then Dr. Bond named it the Lost City of Atlantis Resort."

Celsius adds, "Dr. Bond called the lake of fresh water and the Lost City of Atlantis Resort the perfect synergistic strategy."

"Perfect synergistic strategy," Aristotle says. "Why did Dr. Bond call it that?"

Celsius answers. "Dr. Bond said that without the lake, there would be little interest in the resort, and without the resort, there would be little return on investment. Colonel Tierney said Dr. Bond's perfect synergistic strategy was brilliant. Many leading business journalists said it was brilliant too."

"Was everyone surprised by the success of the resort?" Aristotle asks.

Celsius answers, "Just after I started, I heard Dr. Bond and Colonel Tierney both say they were flabbergasted."

Aqua shakes her head. "In announcements to employees and the press, Dr. Bond and Chrystal, the vice president of public relations, always said the resort was planned."

"Yes, that was the official story," Celsius says. "But in staff meetings, Dr. Bond often mentioned that the success of the resort was an accident."

"How did the resort success happen?" Aristotle asks.

"Every week the public relations department announced new resort offers," Celsius says.

"Did some of the offers fail?"

"Lots did. The public relations department wanted to sell hang-gliding trips off the iceberg. The lawyers shut that down."

"The accidental success of the resort was due to the fact that lots of things were tried and many of them worked. What about the lake on the iceberg? Nitro said only one iceberg was X-rayed. Were other methods of extracting water from icebergs considered?"

"Not that I'm aware of," Nitro says.

"Dr. Bond never mentioned anything other than lakes on icebergs," Celsius adds.

"When the resort started making money, what decisions did Dr. Bond make?"

"Dr. Bond decided to build ten more Atlantis icebergs complete with resorts," Celsius says.

"Dr. Bond delayed draining the lake multiple times," Aqua adds. "Then the iceberg broke and all the fresh water was lost."

Aristotle draws.

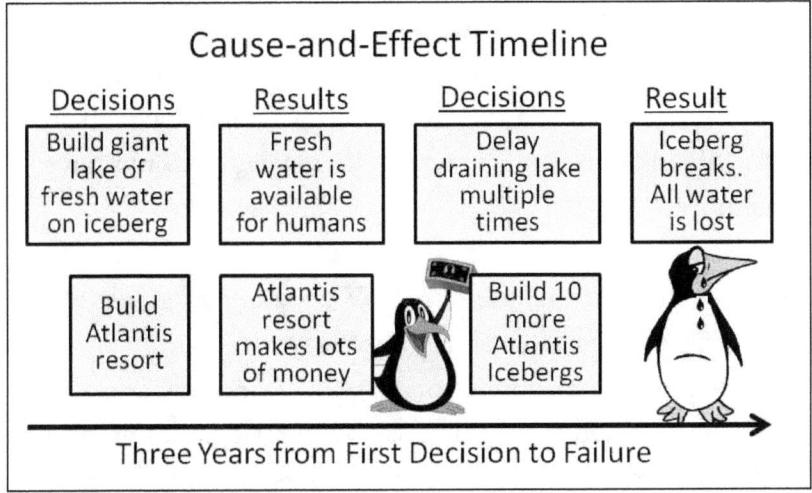

Figure 16-1

Aristotle looks around the room. "Let's take a break. I'd like you all to spend time alone thinking about our discussion. When we reconvene, I want each of you to share the most important thing you learned. Feel free to go to the cafeteria, outside or to your office; wherever you can think clearly. We'll meet back here in half an hour."

Aqua walks outside and watches the waves wash up on the icy beach. The sun is low in the northern sky. She thinks about her swim around Antarctica and how exhilarating it was. Then she thinks about going back inside and sitting in a room with Celsius and Nitro. *I can't wait until this meeting is over so I can get my check and go home.*

Half-an-hour passes quickly, and Aqua returns to the conference room.

"Who wants to start the discussion?"

"I will," Celsius says softly. "Until a few minutes ago, I believed the Atlantis failure was caused by a perfect storm of unforeseeable events. Now I realize it was caused by a combination of a storm that happens fairly regularly and an iceberg that couldn't withstand the stress of the storm in its weakened state. We were lucky no one was killed. We could have understood the stress, and we could have taken responsible action. As Operations Manager, I should have done more."

"Thank you. It takes courage to face up to responsibility when failure occurs. Who wants to go next?"

"I learned the same thing," Nitro says.

"Are there other things you learned?" Aristotle asks.

"Yes. I learned that individuals who raise issues are not troublemakers. They are problem finders, and they should be encouraged, not punished. They are the ones who discover the issues that have to be resolved in order to prevent failure. I wanted to believe Dr. Bond was the perfect penguin with the perfect plan, but he's like the rest of us. He makes mistakes."

"Very good," Aristotle says. "Without problem finders, issues remain undiscovered, and failure can be a perfect storm of unforeseen events. Okay, who's next?"

Frostbite raises his fin. Aristotle nods for him to proceed.

"If Atlantis had been lucky and drained the lake before the iceberg broke, the company would have invested time and money to make ten more Atlantis-like icebergs. I don't have much experience in the business world, but I'm surprised that such a big decision can be made without any more analysis than the fact that the iceberg hadn't failed yet. It's Russian roulette."

"Thank you,' Aristotle says. "Aqua?"

"This whole notion of a perfect synergistic strategy is

baloney. There was no synergy. The two activities were in opposition because for the resort to succeed, the lake could not be drained. How could Dr. Bond make these statements? He was lying!"

"Lying is a strong word," Aristotle says. "Do you have evidence that he lied?"

"I just told you."

"Lying requires willful deceit. Maybe Dr. Bond believed his strategy was synergistic."

"Dr. Bond had to know he was sacrificing customer satisfaction so he could make more profit from the resort."

Aristotle walks to the front of the room. "Aqua's suggestion that Dr. Bond lied about the perfect synergistic strategy and Frostbite's suggestion that Dr. Bond made decisions without proper analysis can only be answered by Dr. Bond. Now, we're going to give Dr. Bond an opportunity to provide answers."

Aqua's jaw drops.

Aristotle continues: "I've known Dr. Bond for years. He was my Chemistry Professor at Penguin University. Last week, I helped him go through a Learning-to-Succeed exercise. I invited him here today to tell you what he learned. He should be in the lobby. I'll be right back."

Aqua's heart skips a beat. She turns to Frostbite. "Did he say Dr. Bond is in the lobby?"

Aqua takes a deep breath and exhales slowly. She remembers "Psychopath" written on the wall. She grabs a marker to cross it out. Too late. Aristotle and Dr. Bond enter the room.

Celsius and Nitro spring to their feet and greet Dr. Bond. They slap fins. Aqua and Frostbite remain in their chairs.

Dr. Bond walks to the ice board at the front of the room and picks up a marker. "I would have preferred to see you all under happier circumstances."

Celsius and Nitro laugh.

Aqua stands and walks to the opposite end of the room by the door, as far away from Dr. Bond as possible. She opens the door a crack for fresh air. She crosses her fins tightly across her chest and breathes slowly.

Dr. Bond writes "Beliefs" on the top of the ice board. At the bottom, he writes "Success / Money."

"What seems like a long time ago, I had an idea that could potentially make heavy water cheaper to manufacture. I was lucky. It worked. It was the subject of my PhD thesis, and I wrote a book about it. I received recognition from my peers and made a little bit of money." He draws an arrow from "Beliefs" to "Success / Money".

Dr. Bond looks at Aristotle, then at Celsius and Nitro, and then at the wall. He sees the word "Psychopath" a few feet from where Aqua is standing.

"My success caused two things. First, it helped my confidence. I started to believe I was smart and my beliefs were right. Second, it increased my desire for greater success. For years, I had tried to figure out how to extract fresh water from icebergs. After a gigantic iceberg broke off of the Ross Ice Shelf, it occurred to me that a lake of fresh water could be created on top of an iceberg and the water could be sold to humans. At the time, I didn't think it was a big deal. In fact, it took months to find anyone who would invest money for me to do it."

Dr. Bond pauses. "Then I met Colonel Tierney. Every time we talked he added a zero to the size of the investment he wanted to make. He introduced me to his

IMAGINE SOLVING THE MOST COMPLEX PROBLEMS

wealthy business partners and the human media networks. He always referred to me as the brains behind the operation. I liked hearing that."

He draws another arrow from 'Success / Money' back to 'Beliefs'.

"I began to believe what the press was saying about me: I was the chosen one, and it was my destiny to save mankind. I believed I could see the future, and I could shape it just the way I wanted. So I delayed draining the lake and decided to build ten more Atlantis-like icebergs."

Dr. Bond writes "Hubris / Self righteousness" next to "Beliefs'. He writes "Fame" next to "Success / Money". Then he draws a large arrow from "Beliefs / Hubris / Self Righteousness" to "Success / Money / Fame" and a large arrow back to "Beliefs / Hubris / Self Righteousness".

He continues: "That was the beginning of the end. I surrounded myself with penguins who told me what I wanted to hear: I was brilliant, the smartest penguin ever, smarter than any human, too. I rejected all bad news, even from competent employees like Celsius and Aqua because it conflicted with my belief that I could do no wrong."

Figure 16-2

Dr. Bond shakes his head. "Atlantis did not deliver one

drop of fresh water to humans, not one drop. But the accidental success of the resort somehow led me to believe I was brilliant, and worse, that I had earned my success. Even after the iceberg broke, I convinced myself the disaster was caused by a perfect storm of unforeseeable events."

Dr. Bond looks at Aristotle. "Did I forget anything?"

Aristotle says softly, "Your name."

"When I published my first book, the publisher, a human, suggested I use a pen name. He didn't want human customers to know I was a penguin because he thought it would hurt sales. He came up with the name, Dr. Hydrogen Bond. At first, it was just going to be my pen name. When I founded Atlantis, I officially changed my name to Dr. Hydrogen Bond. Last week, I changed my name back to Henry Penguin."

Aristotle asks, "Can you tell us what you learned and what you are going to do differently?"

"I learned I'm often wrong but never in doubt. All I really know about is how to make heavy water. When the discussion turns to something else, there is a good chance I'm wrong. And when a CEO is wrong, the effects can be devastating to customers, community, employees, and investors."

He pauses. "What am I going to do differently? I'm going to learn from ideas that are different from mine. I'm going to encourage others to raise issues and admit mistakes. I was doing the opposite. I penalized employees for raising issues and encouraged employees to fabricate good news."

"Can I ask you a couple of questions?" Aristotle says.

"Please," Henry says.

IMAGINE SOLVING THE MOST COMPLEX PROBLEMS

"You mentioned accidental success. What do you mean?"

"I never imagined the resort would make so much money. I built it because Colonel Tierney wanted revenue while I was filling the lake. Then investors and journalists said the resort was a brilliant idea. So I made up the perfect synergistic strategy. It was as if the entire business community was waiting to hear the words: perfect synergistic strategy. I was instantly famous."

"But was the strategy really synergistic?"

"As CEO of Atlantis, part of my job was to promote the company and its strategy. The perfect synergistic strategy worked amazingly well. We had many of the smartest and most powerful penguins and humans in the world at our celebration. Media companies paid more than they pay for the Olympics."

"There's no question that the perfect synergistic strategy was a big money-maker, but weren't the resort and providing fresh water in opposition? Didn't the resort require a big lake of fresh water to attract customers, which meant you couldn't drain the lake and provide water to humans? Didn't you have water for a year-and-a-half without providing any to humans?"

"All I can say is that I was caught in a spiral, the money, the attention."

"Did you tell the truth?"

After a moment, Dr. Bonds says, "Can I have a drink of water?"

"Of course." Aristotle pours Henry a cup of water.

Henry takes a sip, followed by a deep breath.

"I knew I was delaying shipments of water to customers so the resort could make more money." He pauses. "I couldn't accept the crack under the lake because it would ruin everything. And it did." He pauses again, looks down, and whispers: "I knew the two strategies opposed each other. No, I didn't tell the truth."

Henry sighs. "I know I put the lives of humans and penguins in danger. For that I am truly sorry."

Aqua crosses out "Psychopath".

Aristotle looks around. "Thank you, Henry."

Head down, Henry walks slowly toward the door. Just before he leaves the room, Aqua extends her fin. Henry looks at Aqua and extends his fin. Aqua smiles and slaps his fin affectionately. Henry leaves.

After a moment of silence, Aristotle walks to the front of the room. "Any reactions?"

"He actually admitted he lied," Aqua exclaims.

"Unbelievable," Celsius says.

"Wow," Nitro adds.

"Frostbite?" Aristotle says.

"He made those decisions because he believed he could make the future happen just the way he wanted."

"Let's take another break. When we return, we're going to discuss what we've learned thus far, and what we're going to do. Let's resume in twenty minutes."

Aqua walks outside, and sits on a rock on the shore. She feels vindicated. She feels a peacefulness she hasn't felt in a long time. As twenty minutes approaches, she smiles, stands, and turns to walk back inside. As she approaches the building, she feels something she thought she would never feel – sympathy for Dr. Bond.

When everyone is back in the conference room, Aristotle asks, "Who would like to start the discussion?"

Celsius nods. "It took three years to learn Atlantis'

IMAGINE SOLVING THE MOST COMPLEX PROBLEMS

strategy wasn't going to work, and failure occurred well after commitments were made. We have to figure out how to succeed before making commitments, and we have to do it fast."

"Very good. That needs to be a key part of how we move forward. Who's next?"

Nitro raises his fin. "I remember when Dr. Bond first told me to build the resort. Once we started, the resort became the priority, and we delayed draining the lake. Then we never drained the lake. Customers were never satisfied. What started as a short-term project took precedent over customer satisfaction."

"Once an organization starts sacrificing customer satisfaction for short-term profit, it's difficult to stop," Aristotle says. "It rarely ends well. Frostbite, Aqua?"

"I'll go," Frostbite says. "Listening to Dr. Bond say he was often wrong but never in doubt led me to realize that there is a big difference between decision making and problem solving. Although famous as a decision maker, Dr. Bond left a lot to be desired as a problem solver."

"Very insightful," Aristotle says. "Say more about decision making and problem solving."

"Decisions can solve problems, have little or no effect upon problems, or create new problems. Dr. Bond's decisions may have appealed to investors and journalists because they didn't understand the issues associated with his decisions or the assumptions that his decisions relied upon to succeed."

"What do you mean by assumptions?" Celsius asks.

"Dr. Bond kept assuming the iceberg wouldn't break. That assumption turned out to be false."

Aristotle adds: "Important decisions fail when the

assumptions they rely upon to succeed turn out to be false. Assumptions start as suspicions. We have to guard against jumping from suspicions to assumptions without evidence."[4]

"I see that now," Celsius says.

Aristotle turns to Frostbite. "What should the relationship be between decisions and problems?"

"Decision should be the result of effective problem solving."

"Good. That also needs to be part of how we move forward," Aristotle says. "Aqua?"

"Dr. Bond was rewarded with money and fame because his perfect synergistic strategy impressed many influential people and penguins. When rewards and punishment are involved, it's difficult to resist rationalizing what happens in ways that allow us to take credit and avoid blame."

"That's true," Aristotle says. "Dr. Bond also tried to avoid blame by announcing that Atlantis failed because of a perfect storm of unforeseeable events. How can we avoid making up reasons that allow us to take credit and avoid blame?"

"By not blaming each other for making mistakes, raising issues, or not knowing what to do," Aqua says.

"Good. Anything else?"

Frostbite raises his fin. Aristotle nods for him to proceed."

"We can be scientific. By scientific, I mean showing each other evidence that supports our conclusions."

"Very good. Given everything we've learned today, what should we do?"

Celsius stands. "May I draw something?" Aristotle hands him the marker.

"I learned this in business school."

Celsius talks as he draws. "Our vision is 'Iceberg water for humans'. Here are the steps needed to create a strategic plan: Analyze icebergs; explore ideas and select one; plan implementation; test the strategy by exploring stress factors and the ability of our solution to withstand the stress. If the tests are successful, implement the plan and make commitments. Atlantis' strategy failed because feasibility wasn't tested. Feasibility testing would have revealed that a very large lake would weaken the iceberg."

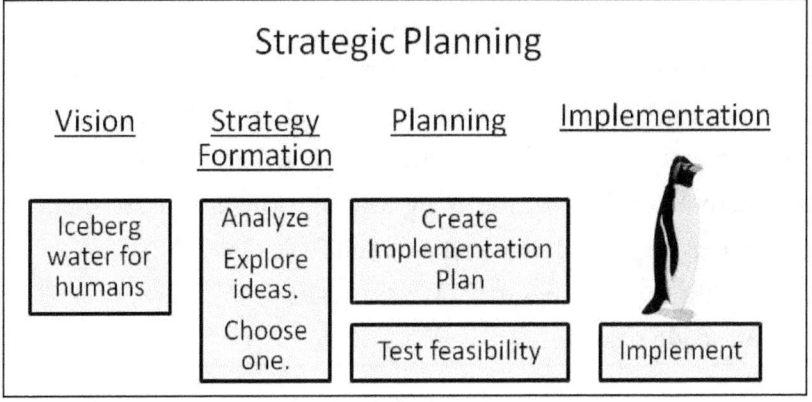

Figure 16-3

"What do the rest of you think?" Aristotle asks.

Frostbite raises his hand. Aristotle nods for him to proceed.

"I worry about choosing a strategy before it's tested."

"I agree," Aqua says. "Once a strategy is chosen and becomes the plan of record, it's difficult to change. In fact, employees can put their careers at risk by suggesting changes to an approved strategy, a lesson I learned at Atlantis."

Aqua turns to Aristotle. "What do you think?

"The step-by-step process Celsius describes is

considered a best practice. It works well if the plan is to do something similar to what was done in the past. Or if the plan is to copy what another organization has done successfully. Or if the organization has a monopoly. But if we want to do something new and complex in an uncertain environment, failure can occur because the strategy is chosen early with little understanding of what customers truly want or how best to serve them."

"That's why we should test feasibility," Celsius argues.

"Feasibility testing, of course, is better than no testing. However, feasibility testing after the strategy is chosen creates pressure to pass the test rather than assess the strengths and weaknesses of an alternative strategy. Consequently, feasibility testing can fail to address an alternative strategy's underlying assumptions and issues. As a result, false confidence can be built."

"What do you suggest?" Celsius asks.

Aristotle draws.

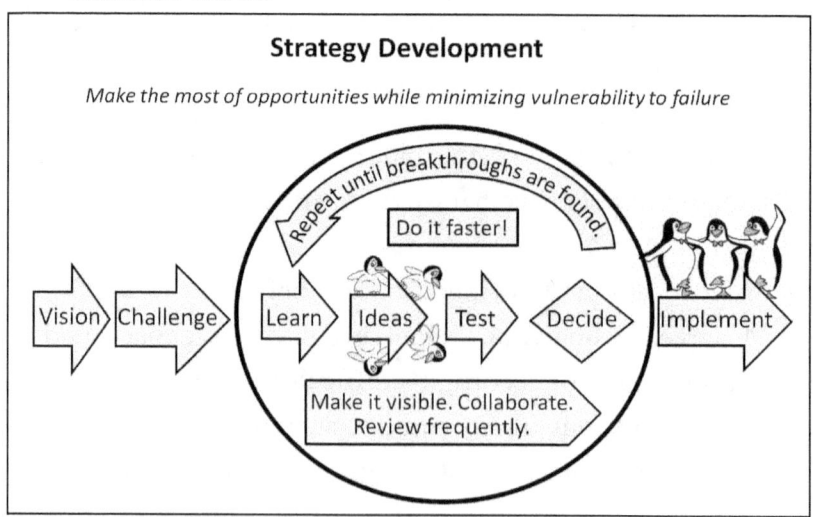

Figure 16-4

"I call it Learn-Ideas-Test-decide.[5] A strategy is a

IMAGINE SOLVING THE MOST COMPLEX PROBLEMS

collection of decisions that together promise to achieve a desired vision and goals. The goal of our strategy is to make the most of opportunities while minimizing vulnerability to failure. Our opportunity is to provide fresh water from icebergs to humans, but in today's complex and uncertain world, there are many ways we can fail."

Aristotle looks around the room. Everyone is engaged. "First, we turn the vision into a challenge because no one can predict the future. Too much uncertainty exists. Our challenge is to find a safe and reliable way to provide fresh water to humans from icebergs. Is everyone okay with that?"

Celsius shakes his head. "That's vague. I was taught that goals should be specific and measurable."

"You're right," Aristotle says. "Goals should be specific and measurable when we want to improve upon the current product, process or result. But when facing complex problems in uncertain environments, specific goals can drive the wrong behavior."

"Dr. Bond's goal of filling the lake with 25 billion gallons of water drove the wrong behavior," Aqua says. "The goal was exceeded but customers were not satisfied."

"That is correct," Aristotle says. "Setting goals is tricky because employees often try very hard to achieve goals, particularly if monetary incentives are involved. In addition to inhibiting customer satisfaction, improper goals can discourage innovation, decrease cooperation among employees, encourage reckless risk-taking, and even lead to unethical behavior."[6]

Aristotle looks at the four and continues: "Challenges are different than goals. Challenges are useful when breakthroughs are needed. We need a breakthrough because we don't know how to safely and reliably provide fresh water to humans from icebergs. Challenges are open-ended and customer-focused."[7]

Celsius stares at Aristotle, looking puzzled. "When will we establish specific and measurable goals?"

"As we learn more, we will establish specific and measurable goals. Let me explain how the learning cycle works. Instead of a sequential process, it's circular. The difficult part is having the discipline to thoroughly evaluate ideas before moving ahead with implementation. Here's a proposed approach."

Aristotle writes on the ice board.

1. What we need to <u>learn</u> before proceeding:
   a. Learn from experiences
   b. Best practices to use in future
   c. Customer requirements
   d. Iceberg physiology
   e. Fresh water extraction methods
   f. Threats, issues, and risks
2. <u>Ideas</u>:
   a. Create potentially viable solutions
   b. Write proposals including issues and assumptions.
3. <u>Test</u> proposals against goals:
   a. Assumptions proposals rely upon to succeed (e.g. will idea delight customers and will customers pay for it?).
   b. Resolutions to issues.
4. <u>Decide</u> whether to move ahead with implementation or repeat the Learn-Ideas-Test-Decide cycle.

"Questions?"

"There are an infinite number of assumptions," Celsius says. "How many do we test?"

"Good question. We identify and test the vital few

assumptions an idea relies upon to succeed. A common cause of failure is false assumptions about what customers want and are willing to pay for. We must understand customer requirements correctly."

"How many times do we repeat the cycle?" Celsius asks.

"This is a learning cycle, which means the more trips through the cycle, the better the alternative solutions become. The cycle is repeated until breakthroughs are found that meet the challenge."

After a moment of silence, Aristotle asks, "What do you think of this circular strategy development approach?"

"I like testing alternatives before making commitments," Aqua says.

"I like that part too," Celsius says. "But I'm worried the process will take too long,"

"Me too," Nitro says. "Humans need water now."

"Do you have experience with this approach?" Aqua asks Aristotle.

"Yes. We operate on this basis in the glacier business."

Celsius shakes his head. "This approach might work in a mature, well understood business, but icebergs are different. We would be embarking upon a research project with no end in sight."

"How can we make this process go faster?" Aristotle asks.

Frostbite raises his fin. Aristotle nods for him to proceed.

"We could meet every day to review progress and decide what to do next. We could also make sure everyone understands the problem by documenting problems and alternative solutions on wall charts."

"I worked for a company that had daily standup meetings and wall charts," Celsius says. "It worked when someone already knew the answer, but it didn't help with hard problems because penguins guessed."

"The purpose of visibility and frequent reviews is to eliminate guessing and enable collaboration that wouldn't happen otherwise," Aristotle says. "That's the foundation for breakthroughs. Are you willing to give this approach a try?"

"I am," Frostbite says. "I like this methodology. It's scientific."

"I'm willing to try this approach for a while," Celsius says, "but I'm concerned it will take too long."

"I'm willing to try too," Nitro adds, "but I have the same concern as Celsius.

"Aqua?" Aristotle says.

"Can I talk to you alone?"

"Yes," Aristotle says. "Celsius, Nitro, Frostbite, thank you very much for your participation."

Aristotle leads Aqua to his office.

Aqua swallows hard. "Is the job you offered me still available?"

A smile spreads across Aristotle's face. "Welcome aboard!"

Part II Summary

Aristotle believes we live in a complex and uncertain world where relying upon the leader or a few experts no longer works. He believes teams are better able to find solutions to complex problems, and his role as a leader is to build high-performance teams.

To begin building a high-performance team, Aristotle conducted a Learning-to-Succeed exercise with Aqua, Celsius, Frostbite and Nitro.[8] A Learning-to-Succeed exercise is a group exercise designed to learn from experiences and to figure out what can be done to achieve better outcomes in the future. A goal of Learning-to-Succeed exercises is to make it safe to discuss sensitive and threatening issues including failures. It is typically two to four hours, with one or two breaks. Breaks provide participants with opportunities to synthesize.

First, Aristotle asked each penguin to create a Five-Why diagram that explains why Atlantis failed. Three different Five-Why diagrams were drawn. Discussing them was insightful. Celsius and Nitro learned that water from the lake had actually weakened the iceberg.

Tempers flared between Aqua and Celsius because Aqua used the Five-Why to blame Celsius and Dr. Bond. Aqua's Five-Why gave Aristotle an opportunity to explain that no one is in a position to know why others did what they did, and that doing so promotes false conclusions.

Aristotle then created a cause-and-effect timeline to help everyone understand which results were caused by which decisions. The timeline and discussion revealed that Atlantis had water to provide to humans for a year-and-a-half, but didn't do so because draining the lake was delayed repeatedly.

After the first break, the four shared what they had learned:

1. Celsius said he learned Atlantis' failure was not caused by a perfect storm of unforeseeable events. It was caused by a combination of a real storm that happens fairly regularly and an iceberg that couldn't withstand the stress of such a storm in its weakened state.
2. Nitro said individuals who raise issues are not troublemakers. They are problem finders. Without them, issues remain unknown and failure really can become a perfect storm of unforeseen events.
3. Frostbite noted that if Atlantis had been lucky and drained the lake before the iceberg broke, the company would have made ten more Atlantis-like icebergs. He compared making important decisions without any more analysis than the fact the iceberg hadn't failed yet with Russian roulette.
4. Aqua accused Dr. Bond of lying when he called his

strategy the perfect synergistic strategy because he had to know that for the resort to succeed, the lake could not be drained.

Aristotle invited Dr. Bond to share what he learned from Atlantis. Dr. Bond said his success, money, and fame, while accidental, led to hubris, self-righteousness, and the belief that he could do no wrong.

When questioned by Aristotle about the perfect synergistic strategy, Dr. Bond admitted that he knew his strategy was not synergistic. He knew he was sacrificing customer satisfaction to make money from the resort. He admitted that he did not tell the truth.

After a second break, the penguins shared what they had learned:
1. Because three years were required to learn Atlantis' strategy wasn't going to work, and failure occurred well after commitments were made., Celsius learned that it is important to figure out how to succeed before making commitments and to do it fast.
2. Nitro pointed out that once Atlantis started sacrificing customer satisfaction for short-term profit, the cycle never stopped, and customers were never satisfied.
3. Frostbite learned there is a difference between decision making and problem solving. He added that Dr. Bond's decisions may have appealed to investors and journalists because they didn't understand the issues associated with his decisions or the assumptions that Dr. Bond's decisions relied upon to succeed.

4. Aqua said that when rewards and punishment are involved, it's difficult to resist rationalizing what happened in ways that allow us to take credit and avoid blame.

Based upon what was learned, Aristotle proposed Learn-Ideas-Test-Decide, an innovation-producing learning-and-decision-making cycle that produces better ideas each time a team makes a trip through the cycle.

Aristotle explained that the first step is to turn the vision into a challenge. Once the challenge is defined, Aristotle said he wants to repeat the Learn-Ideas-Test-Decide cycle until breakthroughs are found that meet the challenge.

Aristotle was pleased with the Learning-to-Succeed results. When it was over, Aqua decided to join Aristotle's company.

Let's see if this approach works.

Part III: Transition

Chapter 17

Habits Die Hard

One Week Later

Aqua arrives in the Lobby at 7:55 Monday morning for her first day with Glacier Fresh Water. "Good morning, Sauna," she says.

"Good morning," Sauna says, handing Aqua an envelope. "When you have a chance, please fill out these forms and return them to me."

Frostbite approaches Aqua with a smile. "There you are. We're meeting in the conference room."

Aqua and Frostbite walk down the hallway and enter the conference room. Celsius and Nitro are already seated next to each other on one side of the table. Aristotle is standing in the front of the room.

"Welcome," Aristotle says. "We're ready to start. Have a seat."

Aristotle begins: "Last week, I spent two days in Penguin City with leaders of government, industry, and academia. The situation in the Middle East is worse. The Prime Minister has asked for our help. While I was there,

Celsius met with a potential customer here."

Aristotle points to the Learn-Ideas-Test-Decide strategy development process on the wall. "Here is the approach we agreed to follow last Monday."

"I've been studying the problem," Celsius announces. "I believe I have a solution." He stands and wirelessly connects his tablet computer to the projector.

Celsius shows the following slide. "The problem definition and root-cause analysis are based upon the Five-Why exercise we did a week ago."

PROBLEM: Prevent Iceberg from Breaking
• **Problem definition:** 　o Atlantis melted the top of an iceberg and captured the water in a large lake for the purpose of draining the lake and providing the water to humans. 　o The iceberg broke and no water was delivered to customers. • Goal: Prevent iceberg from breaking.
Root Cause Analysis – Five-Why: 1. Why did Atlantis fail to deliver water to humans? 　→Because the iceberg broke. 2. Why did the iceberg break? 　→ Because the iceberg was unable to withstand the stress (storm, etc.). 3. Why was the iceberg unable to withstand the stress? 　→ Because water from the lake seeped into the ice and weakened it. 4. Why did the water seep into the ice? 　→ Because there was no barrier to stop it.

Figure 17-1

Celsius points to the fourth question in the Five-Why diagram. "We have the same problem as the machine that stopped because the strainer was missing. The iceberg broke because there was no barrier to stop lake water from seeping into the ice."

Celsius looks at Aristotle. "Let's move on to alternatives." Celsius projects another slide.

EVALUATION OF ALTERNATIVES				
	<u>Alternative</u>	<u>Prevent Water Seeping</u>	<u>Cost</u>	<u>Schedule</u>
1	Build lake as Atlantis did.	Very poor	$0	Fastest
2	Lakebed of solid ice from salt water.	Poor: Ice from salt water melts below 32 degrees	Cheap	Very slow because a very thick layer is required.
3	Lakebed of solid ice from fresh water.	Poor: Ice from fresh water melts at 32 degrees	More than salt water	Slow because a thick layer is required.
4	Lakebed of solid ice from heavy water.	Good: Ice from heavy water melts at 39 degrees.	Quote today	Fast because a thin layer of ice will work.
5	Lakebed of solid ice from heavy water and sawdust.	Excellent: Ice from heavy water melts at 39 degrees. Adding sawdust makes ice stronger than concrete.	Quote today	Fast because a thin layer of ice will work.

Figure 17-2

"I was taught that it's a best practice to have at least three alternatives. I have five. First, we can do exactly what we did at Atlantis, but we know how that turned out.

Second, we could build a lakebed of solid ice made from salt water. This is cheap, but it's very risky because ice made from salt water melts at low temperatures, so the lakebed would have to be very thick. Third, we could build a lakebed of solid ice made from fresh water. This solution is better than salt water, but it would probably still melt."

Celsius smiles. "Fourth, we could build a lakebed of solid ice made from heavy water. Heavy water freezes at thirty-nine degrees, so it won't melt unless the water on top of it is above thirty-nine degrees, which it won't be, because the coldest water will be on the bottom of the lake."

Celsius looks at Aristotle. "Are you ready for the best solution? Adding sawdust makes ice stronger than concrete."

"Sawdust?" Aqua says.

"During WWII, the Allies explored using icebergs as aircraft carriers. They found that the tensile strength of ice increases by 400 percent when sawdust is added. It also melts slower because sawdust is a slow conductor of heat."[9]

Celsius looks at Aristotle and smiles. "Basically we would be building a large swimming pool. We can't fail!"

"Are you sure we can keep the temperature of the bottom of the lake under thirty-nine degrees in the summer?" Aqua asks.

"Good question." Celsius points to the circular strategy diagram. "The next step is testing the idea. At noon today, we leave for the Ross Ice Shelf where we will do experiments. Henry Penguin is lending us a boat with tools. The sawdust arrived last Friday, and it's almost free. This morning, Henry will give us a quote on the heavy water.

IMAGINE SOLVING THE MOST COMPLEX PROBLEMS

We should have a proven solution this week!"

Celsius projects another slide.

TEST AND DECIDE PLAN			
	Action	Who	When
1	Select iceberg.	Celsius, Nitro	Done
2	Obtain heavy water quote from Henry P.	Celsius	Monday am
3	Borrow boat from Henry P. with tools.	Celsius	Monday am
	Experiment to prove it works: a. Dig hole that matches contour of lake. b. Build layer of solid ice made from heavy water and sawdust. c. Measure tensile strength. d. Measure time to build layer of solid ice.	Celsius, Nitro, Frostbite, Aqua	Leave – Monday Return – Thursday
5	Decide to implement.	Aristotle	Friday
6	Secure purchase order for heavy water from Henry P.	Celsius	Friday
7	Begin digging hole for lake on iceberg.	Celsius	Next Monday

Figure 17-3

"Thank you Celsius," Aristotle says. "I see you have given the problem a lot of thought."

"We're ready to go."

"Aristotle," Sauna says, standing in the doorway holding up a cell phone. "You have an important call."

"Excuse me." Aristotle takes the cell phone and leaves the room.

Aristotle returns in thirty seconds. "I'm sorry. I have to leave for Penguin City. Apparently the water crisis is worse."

"Do you have any advice for us?" Aqua asks.

"Think about the issues associated with this plan and the assumptions this plan relies upon to succeed."

"I am," Celsius says. "That's why we're testing the layer of heavy ice with sawdust."

"Anything else?" Aqua asks.

"I want to caution you against jumping to the first solution. We will want to make several trips through the Learn-Ideas-Test-Decide cycle. Sorry, I have to run." Aristotle leaves.

"I have a different idea," Aqua says, 'Let's not pursue lakes on icebergs."

Celsius' jaw drops. "Why in the world would we not pursue lakes on icebergs?"

"It may be too risky, or it may cost too much."

Celsius shakes his head. "We can't succeed by giving up. Leadership is commitment to making something work. Leadership is not giving up."

"You're putting all our eggs in one basket. We're not considering other ideas."

"Tell me the other ideas."

Aqua is silent.

"That's what I thought. All criticism and no solutions."

Celsius' phone rings. He answers. "Yes, I'll be there in one moment." He hangs up. "Dr. Bond, I mean Henry, is here."

Celsius leaves and returns with Henry Penguin. Everyone exchanges pleasantries.

Henry picks up a marker and walks to the ice board. He writes "$6 per gallon." "You can have as much heavy water as you like for six dollars a gallon."

Celsius smiles. "Six dollars a gallon. That's much less than I expected. Thank you."

"I want you to succeed. Send me a purchase order with the quantity you need and the date you need it. You don't have to pay until you start selling water. I'm offering free financing."

Chrystal Penguin arrives at the doorway with Sauna. "Dr. Bond, we have to go."

"Dr. Bond!" Aqua stares at him. "I thought you were Henry Penguin."

"I've taken a new position. I am CEO of a company that sells heavy water. The investors insist I use the name Dr. Hydrogen Bond. If you'll excuse me, I have a plane to catch. I'm meeting with an important customer."

"I was hoping you would accompany us to the Ross Ice Shelf," Celsius says.

"I'd like to, but you can keep the boat with a heated tank of heavy water and equipment for as long as you need."

Dr. Bond walks toward the door.

"Do you mind if I ask you a question?" Aqua says.

"Sure."

"Doesn't production of heavy water require very large amounts of fresh water? Given the worldwide shortage of fresh water, how are you making heavy water?"

"My company already has a large inventory of heavy water. We're looking for customers. That's part of the reason I am able to provide you with such an attractive price."

"Thanks again," Celsius says.

"Thank you. It feels great to be working again and providing a useful service, but I am not looking forward to all the questions from the press. That's why I need Chrystal. Did I tell you I accidently leaked news of the crack under the lake to the media? Me and my big mouth. Don't hesitate to call if you need anything."

Aqua's jaw drops. She stares at Celsius.

Dr. Bond and Crystal leave.

"We leave in one hour," Celsius says and leaves the room. Nitro follows him.

Aqua looks at Frostbite. "This is déjà vu. Celsius is locked onto one idea, and he doesn't want to hear any issues. I'm calling Aristotle."

"I'll see you at the dock."

Aqua calls Aristotle.

"Aristotle, this is Aqua. Do you have a minute?"

"Yes. What is it?"

"We've been talking about Celsius' plan. He hasn't considered any other alternatives, and he doesn't want to hear issues. This feels like Atlantis all over again."

"I'm sorry I had to leave. A common mistake is to only consider the favorite alternative and then do a quick test to build confidence. It's important to let the evaluation determine the best alternative. Let me offer some advice: first, I want you to raise issues, including sensitive ones; second, you might consider doing it one on one so he's not worried about looking bad in front of others; and third, ask him first if he is willing to listen to issues. That will prepare him."

"I'll do that. We're all going to the Ross Ice Shelf to test Celsius' plan."

"I'm going to be in meetings non-stop. I'll call when I get a chance."

Chapter 18

Experimentation

The four penguins board Dr. Bond's boat and head for the Ross Ice Shelf. After an awkward silence, Nitro speaks up. "How thick does the layer of solid ice have to be?"

"I asked Frostbite to look into that last week." Celsius looks at Frostbite.

"I did some research. My initial calculations say the layer of solid ice should be at least five inches thick. But we need to …."

"Five inches! I was thinking two inches at the most. The ice at a hockey rink is less than an inch!"

Frostbite glances at Aqua for support.

"A hockey rink has a concrete floor and cooling pipes," Aqua says. "And an ice resurfacer lays down a new layer of ice for every game. If the heavy ice melts, we're out of luck. It will be too warm to make new ice."

"The heavy ice won't melt because the coldest water will be on the bottom of the lake."

"I still think we should consider other alternatives."

"There you go again."

"Can you tell us about your meeting with the customer?" Aqua says to change the subject.

"I met with Mr. Dalton Cromwell from a company called Hydro for Humanity, located in Christchurch, New Zealand. He wants lots of water as soon as he can get it. I told him we have to be sure we can meet his needs before we make any commitments."

"What do you know about the company?"

"Hydro for Humanity was going to buy a lot of water from Atlantis. The company has a contract with the UN."

"Did Mr. Cromwell tell you know how much water his company wants and when?"

"No, we didn't get to that level of detail."

"Can we find out?"

"Sure. I've got his phone number."

"Over there!" Nitro yells, pointing a spotlight straight ahead. "I put beacons on the five icebergs we selected."

The heavily-lit boat pulls up alongside an iceberg.

"Let's get some sleep," Celsius says. "We'll start first thing in the morning."

The team rises early and starts digging a hole on the iceberg that has the same contour as the proposed lakebed, but smaller. By nightfall, the hole is complete. Too tired to talk, they go to bed.

"Nitro," Celsius says first thing in the morning. "Let's fire up the ice resurfacer."

"The tricky part will be making a layer of ice on the fifteen-degree slope of the lakebed because the water will run down hill," Nitro says.

Nitro starts up the ice resurfacer. It pumps heavy water

from the tank, heats it to eighty degrees Fahrenheit, and sprays it onto the surface of the lakebed. Aqua and Celsius follow behind and sprinkle sawdust on the water. As the water freezes, Frostbite places a few small rods in the ice that he'll use to measure tensile strength.

The four penguins work for the rest of the day with barely a break.

At five o'clock, Celsius turns to Frostbite. "How'd we do?"

"The tensile strength is great. The average depth is an eighth-of-an-inch, and the range of depths is from a tenth to a fourth of an inch."

"Good. Let's talk about the schedule to reach full-scale production. First, we dig the hole for the lake. That will take a week. Second, building a two-inch thick layer of ice will take sixteen shifts, assuming we can build an eighth-of-an-inch per eight-hour shift. At three shifts per day, we need a little over five days. Then we'll have whales push the iceberg to New Zealand. That will take three months. We'll be selling water by the first of November."

"That's great," Nitro said.

"Can I speak with you alone?" Aqua asks Celsius.

"Sure."

Aqua leads Celsius twenty yards away.

"What's up?" Celsius asks.

"There are issues that need to be raised. Are you willing to listen to them?" Aqua looks Celsius straight in the eyes.

"Of course."

"First, building an eighth-of-an-inch of ice per shift for sixteen consecutive shifts requires 100 percent efficiency. One hundred percent efficiency is not realistic. We get nasty storms here. Let's run three shifts but only plan on a fourth of an inch per day. That will give us some margin in case something goes wrong. Then there's the question of thickness. You say two inches. Frostbite says five. I can inspect the lakebed for cracks in the heavy ice every day, but what are we going to do if I find one? We can't fix it without pushing the iceberg back to Antarctica, where it's cold enough to freeze more heavy water. Are we going to shut down?"

Celsius shakes his head. "We built an eighth-inch layer of ice in eight hours, and that was our first try. We'll get better at it. Also, this lake will be much shallower than the Atlantis' lake. I'm not at all worried about one little crack in the heavy ice."

Aqua feels her blood pressure rising. She remembers what Aristotle told her about trying to understand opposing points of view.

"Why do you think it's okay to make the ice two inches thick and plan on everything happening perfectly?"

"Because I think you and Frostbite are being ridiculously conservative. I don't think we need a five-inch layer of ice: We have solid ice underneath; we have a shallow lake; and heavy ice with sawdust has the strength of concrete."

"Here's a realistic schedule," Aqua says. "First, we should plan on two weeks to finish digging the hole. Second, I'd plan four weeks to build a five-inch layer of heavy ice. That puts us at September 1. Third, I've worked with Whale Power a lot, and they typically over-promise and under-deliver. If they say three months, I'd plan on four."

"You're saying we shouldn't count on selling water until January first?" Celsius sighs. "There is no way it will take that long."

"It may be earlier, but I would rather over-deliver than over-commit. The schedule I described also assumes Aristotle makes it his top priority, and provides money and penguins to start immediately."

Celsius is silent for a moment. "Okay. I think we can do much better, and I will tell Aristotle as much. But our conservative schedule shows we can begin full-scale water delivery on January first."

"Fair enough."

Aqua and Celsius return and explain the plan and assumptions to Nitro and Frostbite.

"Frostbite," Nitro says. "How much fresh water do you think this iceberg could produce this summer?"

Celsius' phone rings. "That's probably Aristotle," Celsius says, answering his phone.

"Hello. Yes, this is Celsius. Mr. Cromwell? Yes, I understand the urgency of the situation."

Celsius looks at Aqua. "I'm at the Ross Ice Shelf with three colleagues. We've completed a number of experiments. We've prepared a tentative schedule, but we haven't reviewed it with Aristotle."

"Put him on speaker," Aqua whispers.

"Mr. Cromwell, I'm going to put you on the speaker so my colleagues can hear."

"Can you describe your schedule please?" Dalton Cromwell asks.

All the penguins look at each other.

"Yes," Aqua says. "We have a rough schedule that says we can start providing you with large quantities of water on January first."

"January!" Dalton yells through the phone. "I told you

I need water starting in September!"

Aqua moves closer to the phone. "How much water do you need in September?"

"I need 250 million gallons in September. Then I need two billion in October and four billion in November."

The penguins are quiet.

"Hello," Dalton says. "Are you there?"

"Yes," Aqua says. "We're thinking about how to meet your needs. If you like, we would be happy to review the results of our experiments with you at your convenience."

"Thank you. Perhaps I will take you up on that."

Celsius covers the microphone with his fin and whispers, "Anything else?"

"When would you like your next update?" Aqua asks.

"If you have a breakthrough that provides water in September, please call me immediately day or night."

"We will," Aqua replies.

The four penguins say good-bye.

Aqua stares at Celsius. Her eyes narrow. She turns and marches off shaking her head and mumbling. Celsius follows her.

Aqua quickly turns. "Did you forget to tell us he needs water in September?! Or did you just not consider that important?"

"He said he wanted water in September. He didn't say he would only buy water if we had it in September."

"So you didn't consider it important."

"Humans will need fresh water in November, December, and January. We will always be able to sell water to humans."

"There's an untested assumption."

Celsius takes a deep breath. "I'm sorry I accused you of

leaking the news about the crack under the lake. I jumped to a conclusion, and I was wrong."

"Jumping to conclusions is what you always do, and I'm sick of it!" Aqua marches off.

"I'll tell you one thing. If Dr. Bond was our boss, we'd be selling water in November."

Celsius' phone rings. "What now?" He answers his phone.

"Yes. ... Mr. Cromwell! Yes, I mean no. I mean yes. We would be happy for you to come. ... We will see you tomorrow." Celsius hangs up.

"Dalton Cromwell is coming here to the Ross Ice Shelf so he can personally see what is happening. He's bringing the Chairman of the Board."

"When?" Aqua asks.

"Tomorrow at noon. They're arriving by helicopter."

Chapter 19

Apocalypse Appears Certain

Just before noon, a helicopter lands on the iceberg. The penguins walk quickly to the helicopter as a woman pilot and a male passenger step out.

The humans introduce themselves as Dalton Cromwell, President of Hydro for Humanity, and Meredith Macbeth, CEO and Chairman of the Board.

"Thank you for inviting us here," Meredith says.

Aqua walks with Meredith on the slick heavy ice. "I've always wanted to walk on an iceberg," Meredith says. "My hobby is mountain climbing." She turns and looks back at Dalton. "Dalton, are you coming?"

"Yes." Dalton walks gingerly down the embankment. "I should have brought a snowmobile."

The penguins show Meredith and Dalton the ice made from heavy water and sawdust and describe the schedule. Meredith and Dalton ask lots of questions.

After a half-an-hour, Meredith says: "Thank you for showing us your work. I'm glad you are taking the time to

IMAGINE SOLVING THE MOST COMPLEX PROBLEMS

solve problems before making commitments. Let me tell you about our company. We entered the fresh water business ten years ago to address the biggest problem facing the human race. Over one third of the world's human population suffers from the lack of fresh water. Ten thousand people die every day, mostly children.[1] Most of our water is provided to people in Africa, Asia, South America, and the Middle East. We have a contract with the United Nations to provide water on its behalf."

"Can you tell us what is driving the need for so much fresh water in September?" Aqua asks.

"We need water in September to deliver in October. Starting in October a million people in the Middle East will no longer have access to fresh water. The number of people without fresh water will grow rapidly in November and December. The entire region is facing its worst draught on record. The Turkish mountains that feed the Tigris and Euphrates rivers recorded their least precipitation ever last winter. That means Turkey, Syria, and Iraq all face extreme water shortages. Syria, which is downstream from Turkey, has told Turkey that any attempt to withhold water will be considered an act of war. Iraq, which is downstream from both Syria and Turkey, has sent the same message to Turkey and Syria."

"Over a hundred million people in those three countries depend upon those mountains for water," Dalton adds. "And it gets worse. The Sea of Galilee is at its lowest level ever. Israel, Jordan, and Syria have fought over that water before."

Meredith continues: "Oil-producing countries have reduced oil production in order to free up fresh water for their citizens. The price of oil has doubled, which has raised the price of all products that rely on petroleum, including food. High oil prices hit poor people the hardest."

Dalton adds: "In the last week, militaries have assembled along the borders between Iraq and Syria, Syria and Turkey, and Israel and Jordan. America has half its Navy in the Persian Gulf to make sure it stays open to oil tankers. China has sent battle ships too. The situation is a powder keg ready to explode."

"We provide water to people who rely on it to live," Meredith says. "If you make a commitment to us, we treat it as a guarantee. We planned to purchase half the water from Atlantis. Its failure has caused a massive shortfall."

"I'm really sorry, but we don't know how to meet your needs," Aqua says.

"Thank you. Now I have the unpleasant task of telling the United Nations I do not have water needed for the Middle East." Meredith and Dalton turn and begin walking up the embankment.

Celsius follows Meredith and Dalton. "If we provide water according to the rough plan we outlined, are you interested in buying it?"

Meredith turns. "Your plan starts delivery in January and grows from there?"

"We might be able to provide water sooner, maybe early November."

"Let me be perfectly clear. I need a commitment, not a maybe. Atlantis changed its delivery date four times, and we didn't receive a single drop. We need water in September. If we don't receive it, humans will starve! Militaries will fight for water. Water has been the cause of conflict for thousands of years. The city of Rome was laid

IMAGINE SOLVING THE MOST COMPLEX PROBLEMS

to waste in 537 AD because the Goths destroyed the aqueducts that brought water into the city. The Dutch have opened the dikes and flooded their low lands several times to stop enemies.[10] To answer your question, we will buy water from you if we still need it. But we're working day and night to find water for September."

"We will continue to look for a September solution," Aqua says.

"If you find a way, call me or Dalton immediately." They return to their helicopter and take off.

"What now?" Nitro asks.

"Our heavy water experiments were successful," Celsius says. "We head back."

"I'm going to swim back," Aqua says.

"I'll join you," Frostbite says.

They all pack up the boat. Celsius and Nitro leave.

Before Aqua and Frostbite set off, Aqua's phone rings. It's Celsius. "Aristotle just called and said he wants to have a meeting at 3:00 tomorrow afternoon. Do you two want a ride?"

"It's at least an eight-hour swim," Aqua says.

"I could use the exercise," Frostbite says.

"Thanks," Aqua tells Celsius. "We're going to swim."

Chapter 20

Pushing for Implementation

"I'm glad you're all here," Aristotle says. "Meredith and Dalton flew into Penguin City yesterday afternoon after they met with you. Meredith informed us that she does not have a source for water in September, so there is nothing to prevent the water crisis."

"The good news is that our heavy water experiments were successful," Celsius says. "Nitro and I created a list of alternatives." Celsius projects a slide.

"We recommend alternative number one because we can start delivering water in the November. But we have to start right away."

Aristotle walks up to the screen. "It costs $3.4 million to build a two-inch layer of ice under the lake with enough capacity for one day of water. Is one day enough capacity?"

"Yes."

"Do you think building a two-inch layer of ice from heavy water and sawdust under a lake is safe and reliable?"

"Absolutely. It's a swimming pool."

	Alternative	Total Cost: water, fuel, labor	Probability of success	Schedule – First Water Delivery
1	Two-inch thick layer using heavy water and sawdust.	Heavy water: $3.3 million Total: $3.4 million	Excellent	November
2	Five-inch thick layer using heavy water and sawdust.	Heavy water: $8.25 million Total: $8.4 million	Excellent + margin of safety	December – January
3	12-inch layer ice using sea water and sawdust.	Total: $40K	Unreliable	Too slow to estimate.
4	12-inch layer using fresh water and sawdust.	Fresh water: $10,000 Total: $100K	Medium	March – late summer
Assumptions: • Capacity – 5 billion gallons per month • Lake holds a day's supply of water – 167 million gallons • Water is pumped continuously into tankers			

Figure 20-1

"Very good," Aristotle says, and points to the circular strategy formation diagram. "The next step is deciding what to do. Before making decisions, I like to make all the information visible. Celsius, I would like you to prepare a detailed plan for moving forward, including how much water can be delivered by month. Aqua, I would like you to prepare a document showing Hydro for Humanity's requirements by month. I'd like to review both in our meeting first thing Monday morning. Both documents will be placed on the wall, so please use two-foot-by-three-foot pieces of paper and make them clear and concise. Any questions?"

"Why do you want large documents on the wall?" Celsius asks.

"So we can stand in front of them and discuss the information. We're going to solve this problem together, collaboratively, with issues visible to everyone. I believe all of us are smarter than any one of us. Also, I want you all to feel responsible for solving the problem of how to safely and reliably provide fresh water to humans using icebergs. Any other questions?"

"Can we move forward with a purchase order for heavy water from Dr. Bond?" Celsius asks.

"We will make that decision on Monday."

"The clock is ticking," Celsius says. "The sooner we start building a layer of heavy ice, the sooner we can deliver fresh water."

"I realize not moving into implementation is uncomfortable."

Aristotle's phone rings. "Sorry I have to take this call. I'll see you all Monday."

Chapter 21

Making It Visible

The team gathers in the conference Monday morning at eight o'clock. Aqua and Celsius brought wall charts.

"I'd like to start by reviewing the one-page documents," Aristotle says. "Aqua, let's start with yours. Please attach your document on the wall."

Aqua tapes her chart to the wall. "I called Meredith Friday afternoon. These are the numbers she gave me. The number of humans served is based upon the assumption that a family of five, two adults and three children, need forty gallons of water per day or 1,200 gallons each month."

Aristotle walks over to the document and reads it.

"Two cents per 1,000 gallons?" Celsius says. "We were planning on twice that much at Atlantis."

"The revenue number is from Meredith." Aqua turns to Aristotle. "Is two cents per 1,000 gallons what you would expect?"

"It's close to what we sell water for."

CUSTOMER: Hydro for Humanity

- Hydro for Humanity has a contract with the UN to provide fresh water to humans who need it in Africa, Asia, South America, and the Middle East.
- The Middle East is facing an acute crisis beginning in October.
- Hydro for Humanity will only discuss a plan that starts water delivery in September.
- Hydro for Humanity demand:

Month	Fresh water (gallons)	People served assuming family of 5*	Estimated revenue ($0.02 per 1000 gallons)
September	250 million	1 million	$5,000
October	2 billion	8.3 million	$40,000
November	4 billion	16.7 million	$80,000
December	6 billion	25 million	$120,000
January	6 billion	25 million	$120,000
February	6 billion	25 million	$120,000
March	6 billion	25 million	$120,000

* Family of 5 (2 adults, 3 children) need 40 gallons of fresh water per day or 1,200 gallons per month.

Figure 21-1

"I have a question," Celsius says. "If we can provide more water in a given month, will they buy it?"

"I don't know," Aqua replies.

"Why does the demand level out at six billion gallons per month?" Nitro asks.

Aqua looks at Aristotle. "Do you want me to follow up on all these questions?"

IMAGINE SOLVING THE MOST COMPLEX PROBLEMS

"Yes, and I'd like you to add a section for next steps and list whatever you are going to do next."

Aristotle turns to Celsius. "Let's see what you have."

Celsius attaches a document to the wall next to Aqua's.

PROJECT: Fresh Water Lake on Layer of Heavy Water and Sawdust

- Build two-inch layer of solid ice made from heavy water and sawdust on lakebed.
- Lake is drained every day.
- Estimated water capacity: 5 billion gallons per month.
- Schedule:

Task:	Complete	Who
Secure heavy water at great price - $3.3 million.	Today	Celsius
Project staffing complete.	July 22	Celsius
Equipment in place to dig hole for lake.	July 22	Nitro
Hole for lake complete.	July 29	Nitro
Two-inch layer of ice made of heavy water and sawdust done.	August 5	Celsius
Operations equipment, housing, etc. on iceberg.	August 5	Frostbite
Whales begin pushing iceberg to Christchurch.	August 5	Aqua
Canals built.	Sept. 31	Nitro
Begin filling lake.	Oct. 1	Nitro
Iceberg arrives in Christchurch.	Nov. 1	Aqua
Begin water delivery.	Nov. 1	Celsius
Deliver 1 billion gallons.	Nov. 30	Celsius
Deliver 3 billion gallons.	Dec. 31	Celsius
Deliver 5 billion gallons.	Jan. 31	Celsius
Deliver 5 billion gallons.	Feb. 28	Celsius
Deliver 3 billion gallons.	March 31	Celsius

Figure 21-2

Celsius looks at Aristotle. "This is an aggressive schedule. But we should be aggressive. Humans are desperate for water. If we start now, we can begin delivering water on November 1. Any questions?"

"Have you identified issues that need to be resolved and assumptions this idea relies upon to succeed?" Aristotle asks.

"Yes. This plan assumes we start today by securing heavy water. This plan assumes we execute: we dig the hole in one week; we build the two-inch layer of ice in less than one week; whales push the iceberg to Christchurch in three months; we begin filling the lake on October 1; and we keep the water on the bottom of the lake below thirty-nine degrees. There are issues too. To prevent water from getting under the layer of heavy ice and sawdust, Nitro wants to pump water from incoming canals directly into the lake. The issues and assumptions are all manageable. This plan is executable."

"Can you add a section to your document called issues and assumptions?"

"Sure."

"Did you discuss a conservative schedule?"

"Yes," Aqua says. "We allow two weeks to dig the hole, four weeks to build a five-inch layer of heavy ice with sawdust, and four months for the whales to push the iceberg to Christchurch. Water delivery starts on January first."

Aristotle attaches a blank two-foot-by-three-foot piece of paper to the wall. "I'm going to draw a diagram that shows the gap between what Hydro for Humanity requires and what we can deliver under the aggressive and conservative schedules. Please check my work."

IMAGINE SOLVING THE MOST COMPLEX PROBLEMS

He carefully draws.

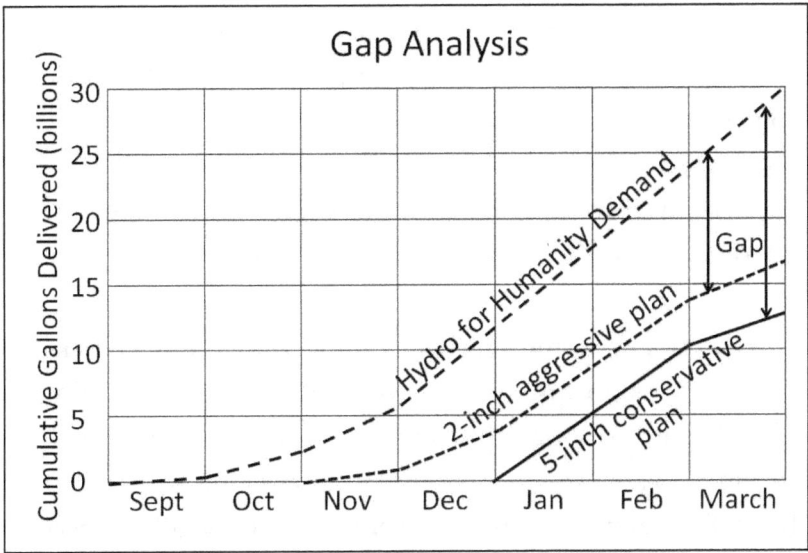

Figure 21-3

Frostbite walks over to the diagram. "It's accurate."

"Does the gap diagram provide insight?" Aristotle asks.

Frostbite points to the March lines. "The gap diagram reveals that the gap increases faster when summer ends because building a lake on an iceberg only produces water during warm months."

Celsius shakes his head. "We'll push the iceberg further north for the winter. Auckland has mild winters."

Celsius walks over to his wall chart and writes, "5 billion" in the row showing March 31 water delivery. "These issues are all manageable."

Aristotle points to the Learn-Ideas-Test-Decide chart. "You've made a lot of progress: you've proposed one solution; you've performed some testing; and you know what a potential customer wants. You've also made what you know visible. Now we decide what to do next."

"I think we should move forward with a lakebed of ice made from heavy water and sawdust," Celsius says. "We've proven we can build it. We'll begin water delivery in November."

"I agree," Nitro says.

"The decision step often generates disagreement," Aristotle says. "Remember, disagreements are an opportunity to learn and generate better ideas."

Aqua points to the gap diagram. "If our goal is to make the most of opportunities and avoid vulnerability to failure, Celsius' plan fails on both counts. Neither the two-inch aggressive plan nor the five-inch conservative plan meets Hydro for Humanity's requirement to begin water delivery in September. The two-inch aggressive plan also sacrifices safety and reliability for cost and schedule."

"It's better than doing nothing," Celsius argues.

"The gap diagram shows that building a lake on an iceberg is not the way to go," Aqua says.

"We can't just sit here."

"Maybe failing is okay with you, but I've had enough Iceberg Down situations."

"Let's get everyone's thoughts," Aristotle says. "Frostbite?"

"I think we learned a lot from Atlantis and the heavy water experiments, but I suspect there are better solutions out there. Maybe we can find a way to meet Hydro for Humanity's requirements safely and reliably."

"Thank you for your input," Aristotle says. "I'd like to spend this week going back through the Learn-Ideas-Test-Decide cycle and try to figure out how to meet Hydro for Humanity's requirement to begin water delivery in September."

IMAGINE SOLVING THE MOST COMPLEX PROBLEMS

"September!" Celsius protests. "We know we can't melt ice in time to deliver water in September. It's the middle of winter, for crying out loud!"

Aqua rolls her eyes.

Celsius glares at Aristotle. "Building a lake on an iceberg is hard enough. Now you've added the impossible goal of delivering water in September. Adding difficult new requirements causes projects to fail. It's called scope creep."

Celsius looks at Nitro.

Nitro clears his throat. "I agree with Celsius."

"I realize it's difficult to consider other ideas when you have a lot of experience with one way of doing things," Aristotle says.

Frostbite raises his hand. Aristotle nods for him to proceed.

"I like the documents on the wall. They're easy to understand, particularly the gap document."

"I don't like what I see," Nitro says.

"Why not?" Aristotle asks.

"It's depressing because the gap is so big."

"Sometimes the truth is hard to accept. Would you rather know the truth about a problem or pretend there is no problem?"

"I'll feel better when the problem is solved. Working here is a lot different from Atlantis. Dr. Bond always told us things were going amazingly well."

"Any other thoughts?" Aristotle asks.

"Yea," Celsius says. "We're wasting time making wall charts of the obvious. We should be on the iceberg right now digging a hole and laying down a layer of ice made from heavy water and sawdust. We know what we have to do, and we should get on with it."

"I realize that meeting Hydro for Humanity's requirements is not easy."

"Can we at least secure our supply of heavy water from Dr. Bond? I'd hate to lose the price he gave us last week."

"I'm not ready to make that investment. The goal for this week is to look for ways to close the gap. When you come up with an idea, write it on the wall. We have plenty of wall space in this room. Let's plan on meeting here every morning at eight o'clock."

Aristotle takes a deep breath. "I'd like to thank Aqua and Celsius for preparing wall charts."

Aristotle's phone rings. "I have a phone call with the Prime Minister of Penguin Land. She wants a status of what we can do. If you don't mind leaving, I'd like to call her from this room so I can tell her exactly what the situation is."

"I'm starving," Aqua says. "I'm going to the cafeteria for some fish."

"I'll join you," Frostbite says.

"I have to make a phone call," Celsius says and leaves. Nitro follows him.

Aqua and Frostbite walk to the cafeteria, where they retrieve fresh fish from the refrigerator and sit down facing the television.

"It's time for the water report. This is Walter Penguin. The situation has deteriorated further in the Middle East. Gunfire has erupted along borders as countries protect their water supplies. The United States and China have positioned naval fleets at the Strait of Hormuz, a twenty-mile-wide waterway that transports one-fourth of the world's oil. It's twilight for the human race, as it appears

IMAGINE SOLVING THE MOST COMPLEX PROBLEMS

badly needed fresh water will not arrive in time."

The television starts beeping.

The announcer says, "We have a breaking story. Dr. Hydrogen Bond, the former CEO of Atlantis, has been arrested for illegally trafficking heavy water. Once again the most celebrated penguin of our time has brought shame on all of us in Penguin Land."

Over the public address system is heard, "Will Celsius Penguin, Aqua Penguin, Nitro Penguin, and Frostbite Penguin please report to the lobby immediately."

When they arrive in the lobby, they find it filled with police officers.

A tall man approaches. "My name is Jean Chirac from the International Criminal Police Organization. You may have heard of us as INTERPOL." He shows Aqua his badge. "Please come with me."

The penguins are escorted out to a small boat that takes them from the lagoon to a large ship moored out in the ocean. Each is escorted into an interrogation room.

Chapter 22

Mad Emperor's Disease

An hour later, the interrogation is still under way. An INTERPOL officer is drilling Aqua with questions, "Did you know heavy water is a controlled substance?"

"No, I did not."

"Did you know Dr. Bond owes Colonel Tierney a lot of money?"

"No, I did not."

"Did you know Colonel Tierney has ties to rogue governments that have been trying to obtain nuclear weapons illegally?"

"Absolutely not. None of this makes sense to me."

"Let me explain. Heavy water allows normal uranium, right out of the ground, to be used in nuclear reactors to generate electricity. A by-product is weapon-grade plutonium! That's how several countries have developed nuclear weapons. Now we'll start from the top. When did you first meet Dr. Hydrogen Bond?"

IMAGINE SOLVING THE MOST COMPLEX PROBLEMS

****

Exhausted, Aqua walks slowly back toward the lobby. Frostbite is waiting for her.

"How did it go?" Aqua asks.

"Not too bad. Because I only met Dr. Bond two weeks ago, we didn't have much to talk about."

They walk inside and hear voices from Aristotle's office. They enter and see that Celsius and Nitro are there already.

"You okay?" Aristotle asks.

Aqua nods. "Sounds like Dr. Bond is back to his old tricks."

"INTERPOL confiscated our tank of heavy water for evidence," Nitro says. "We don't even have a sample to experiment with."

"We've got nothing," Celsius says. "No plan, no ideas."

"This is a setback," Aristotle says. "Let's not become discouraged. We will solve this problem."

Aristotle glances at his watch.

"Are you going to be around for a while?" Aqua asks.

"I'm leaving for Penguin City in five minutes. Henry will be turned over to the Penguin Police. I hope to speak with him tonight. Go ahead and have the eight o'clock meeting tomorrow without me. Feel free to call if you need anything."

****

Aristotle sits facing the glass. He has been waiting for nearly an hour. Finally, a police officer escorts Dr. Bond to a chair on the opposite side of the glass.

Dr. Bond sits down. The two pick up phones on each

side of the glass.

"Aristotle, my old friend. You look well."

"Henry, are you all right?"

"I could use a decent meal, but other than that I can't complain."

"What's going to happen to you?"

"My lawyers say I will be out in a day or two. I'm glad you came. Let me bring you up to speed. After the meeting at your factory, I called Celsius and told him to use heavy water and sawdust to make a layer of solid ice under the lake. If you do that, icebergs will produce fresh water for years. INTERPOL never should have taken your sample of heavy water. My lawyers are clearing the way for me to resume selling. Within a day or two, we can proceed with a purchase order."

"Can we back up a little? Why were you arrested?"

"This whole thing is a mistake. Everything I did was legal."

"The television news says you were arrested for illegally trafficking heavy water."

"We all know television news is an oxymoron. They're lying to increase their ratings. My heavy water process is one of the greatest innovations in history. It will allow you to provide fresh water to starving humans. It will allow free countries to protect themselves against tyrants and terrorists."

"But I heard ...?"

Dr. Bond cuts Aristotle off. "I've assembled the best legal team in the country. I'm going to sue INTERPOL for wrongful arrest. They will regret the day they messed with Dr. Hydrogen Bond. Then I can fulfill my destiny to save mankind."

IMAGINE SOLVING THE MOST COMPLEX PROBLEMS

"I'm confused. What happened to Henry Penguin?"

"Who?"

"What happened to everything you learned from Atlantis?"

"I learned heavy water is a gold mine. I learned it is my destiny to save mankind. It's what Dr. Hydrogen Bond was born to do. I played along with your little game of admitting mistakes and learning from experiences. But now it's time to get serious."

"Excuse me?"

"I said it's time to get serious. Humans need water. You can provide it using my solution. You need to get on with it."

"I'm not sure that's the best way to go."

"Nonsense! Did you know Celsius has called me three times since Friday? He wants to know why you can't make a decision. He'll execute for you, but you have to make the decision to start."

"I want my team to study other options and take ownership for finding the best solution."

"Your team?" Dr. Bond laughs. "You'll be dead and long forgotten before your team finds a solution."

"I disagree."

"You're embarrassing! Let me tell you how the world works. The world is divided into two groups: the trivial many who do what they're told, and the vital few who do the thinking and decide what the trivial many will do."

"I believe otherwise."

"Don't insult my intelligence by telling the hired help to raise issues, suggest ideas, and admit mistakes. Tell them what to do, and tell them they will be part of something great by doing it. Create a sense of urgency. That's how you give them purpose. The trivial many need purpose, or they waste their lives away."

Aristotle shakes his head.

Dr. Bond continues: "I'm throwing you a rope here. Use my heavy water to save the humans. I'll share the credit with you if that's what you're worried about."

After a pause Dr. Bond adds, "If you don't, I will."

Aristotle straightens his shoulders. "If you're so great at doing all the thinking and making all the decisions, why did Atlantis break and lose all its fresh water."

"I'll tell you why! Because of that little trouble-maker, what's her name?"

"Aqua?"

"Yes Aqua. She's great at finding problems, but she doesn't bother to solve problems. If she would have done her job, I would have delivered the water and this crisis would be over!"

"That's absurd."

"You need to fire her and hire more penguins like Celsius and Nitro. They get the job done."

"Henry, I hope someday you learn there is more to leadership than arguing and arrogance."

A police officer approaches Aristotle. "Are you Aristotle Penguin?"

"Yes."

"There is someone here to see you."

"Henry," Aristotle says. "I wish you well."

"Call me about the heavy water. Remember. My name is Dr. Bond, Dr. Hydrogen Bond!"

Aristotle stands and follows the policeman down the hallway.

"Aristotle Penguin," a deep, clear voice calls out from

behind Aristotle.

"Yes, I'm Aristotle Penguin."

A short penguin roughly the same age as Aristotle extends his fin. "I'm Sigmund Penguin, head of the Psychology Department at Penguin University. Do you have a few minutes?"

"Yes."

Sigmund leads Aristotle into an empty room. They both sit.

"I understand you are a close friend of Dr. Hydrogen Bond," Sigmund says.

"I wouldn't say we're close, but I've known him for many years. I just spoke with him."

"How did you find him?"

"Surprisingly confident and certainly not apologetic. He said the whole thing is a misunderstanding."

"I assure you it is not a misunderstanding. I've also known Dr. Bond for years. I've studied his behavior closely since he became famous." He pauses. "Dr. Bond suffers from what we call Mad Emperor's Disease."[11]

"Mad Emperor's Disease?"

"The clinical name is egophrenia.[11] Dr. Bond is incapable of self-reflection. Even though Atlantis failed and he's been arrested for illegally trafficking heavy water, he doesn't think he did anything wrong. He invents reasons that free him from blame. He interprets all his experiences as evidence that support his beliefs."

Aristotle nods. "After the Atlantis iceberg broke, I led Dr. Bond through a learning-to-succeed exercise. He was insightful, apologetic, and committed to change. He even said he changed his name back to Henry Penguin. Then a week later, I found out he was Dr. Hydrogen Bond again,

CEO of a company that sells heavy water. He played along with me for the sole purpose of selling me heavy water."

"Egophreniacs will say anything to gain your trust. They are charming and persuasive. They must persuade others their intention is noble. They feed on admiration, so they surround themselves with individuals who tell them how great they are."

"He just told me it's his destiny to save mankind. Does he believe what he says?"

"Absolutely. Egophreniacs believe their mission is just, their decisions are sound, and their plans perfect, no matter how wrong their actions are. The media is often an unwitting accomplice because egophreniacs thrive on the limelight. They are news makers."

"Is egophrenia common?"

"It's fairly common among the rich and famous, overpaid executives, and politicians. Very bad things can happen when an individual in a position of power has Mad Emperor's Disease. It's the dark side of our nature."

"Will he ever recover?"

"Yes. We have reformed dozens of individuals with egophrenia. After a short stint in jail, he will be given the opportunity to help others, either in a hospital or with the disabled or disadvantaged. Soon he will prefer to serve others instead of only himself."

Chapter 23

Had Enough

It's late and Aqua is restless. She decides to call Aristotle and is relieved when he answers. "I know it's late," Aqua says, "but I really need to talk to you."

"What's on your mind?"

This is a tough conversation to have over the phone.

"I've been thinking about how things are going. I don't know what your expectations are, but I don't see us making progress. Do you agree?"

Aqua waits for Aristotle to say something.

"I think we're just starting. Tell me more."

"Last week with Celsius was déjà vu. He behaved exactly the same way he did at Atlantis. He didn't have a clue what Dalton Cromwell wanted, and he charged off with his heavy ice and sawdust idea and wouldn't listen to anyone. He thinks we can deliver water in November, but he's counting on 100 percent efficiency, which is not realistic. I took your advice and pulled him aside and asked him if he wanted to hear issues. He listened, but then he told Meredith we might be able to deliver water in November. I lost my temper and let him have it. Look, he's not going to change. He's decided he knows what we need to do and we should get on with it. You heard him."

"Yes, I heard him."

"Now Dr. Bond is arrested, which is good, because he's a menace to society. He's not going to change either."

Aqua takes a deep breath. "Starting tomorrow, I would like to take a leave of absence until it's time to start up the greenhouse."

Aristotle is silent.

"Aristotle, are you there?"

"I'm sorry. Can I call you back in the morning? I have to take another call."

"Can you call before work?"

"Yes, I will call at seven o'clock. Good night."

I wonder if he really had another call or he just didn't want to talk. If he doesn't give me the leave of absence, I'm going to quit. Either way, starting tomorrow, I'm not working with Celsius.

Part III Summary

Aristotle told Aqua, Celsius, Frostbite and Nitro that he plans to turn them into a high-performance team. He defined a high-performance team as a team whose performance is high enough to quickly find breakthroughs to the most complex problems. That's the easy part, a definition in terms of desired outcomes.

Aristotle said the keys are to learn from experiences, raise issues, suggest ideas, admit mistakes, make everything visible, and learn from disagreements. The conference room walls were covered with documents.[12]

But that approach didn't work with Dr. Bond. He played along for the sole purpose of selling Aristotle heavy water. After he was arrested, he mocked Aristotle for suggesting that employees be encouraged to offer ideas, raise issues, and admit mistakes. Dr. Bond claimed he was uniquely qualified to do the thinking and make the decisions for others.

Aristotle told the four penguins that disagreements were a source of learning that results in better ideas. But instead, disagreements resulted in resentment and paralysis.

Get to the new world

Aqua, Celsius, Nitro and Frostbite are a team in transition. They're in the Neutral Zone.[13]

They have one foot in the new world and one in the old. The new world is visibility and collaboration, but collaboration isn't happening because their behavior is rooted in the old world of Atlantis.

Celsius is still doing what Dr. Bond tells him to do, and he's frustrated that Aristotle did not give him the go ahead to build a lakebed with ice made from heavy water and sawdust. Aqua is still finding issues with whatever Celsius wants to do, and Celsius doesn't want to hear them. Nitro always sides with Celsius. Frostbite always sides with Aqua.

Aristotle can't stay in the Neutral Zone too long because frustration is boiling over. Any commitment to finding a safe and reliable way to extract water from icebergs that existed when the team started has vanished. Celsius wants to relax the goals. Aqua wants to throw in the towel.

Has Aristotle overestimated his ability to change behavior? He's running out of time to build a high-performance team capable of saving the human race.

Part IV: Defensive versus Collaborative Responsibility

Chapter 24

Assumptions Drive Behavior

Aqua hardly slept. She spent the night mulling over her options. She wants to work at Glacier Fresh Water but she does not want to work with Celsius. She likes the idea of Glacier Fresh Water paying for her college courses and tutoring her. If she quits, she'll have to take out loans and find a part-time job. But her first priority is to get away from Celsius and the iceberg business. And she fully expects Aristotle will try to talk her into staying.

Aqua's phone rings.

"Good morning," Aristotle says in a cheery voice.

"Thanks for calling early."

"My pleasure. First, I appreciate your openness."

"Thank you. Are you going to approve my leave of absence?"

"If it's what you really want, I'll support it. But I'd like you to give the iceberg challenge more time."

"Sorry, I've made up my mind."

"Could you do me the favor of listening for a moment?"

Here it comes. "I guess."

"Thank you. After years of frustration, I figured out that to a large degree I create my own reality. What this means is: only you can create a déjà vu for yourself, and only you can stop déjà vus from happening."

Aqua sighs.

"A high-performance team is created when someone steps up and changes his or her behavior such that others respond differently."

"Are you telling me not to raise issues?"

"No, not at all. I absolutely want you to raise issues."

"I'm trying to take responsibility for preventing another disaster. Didn't we all agree that Atlantis' failure was not caused by a perfect storm of unforeseeable events? I do not want to face any more Iceberg Down situations because Celsius refuses to see them coming."

"I realize you're trying to do what's right. I want to prevent disasters, too. But there are two types of responsibility. There is responsibility that is defensive and responsibility that is collaborative. Many of us spend lots of time figuring out how to defend ourselves and our organization against others whom we perceive as threats. That's defensive responsibility. Although defensive responsibility may succeed in stopping threats, it's unlikely to lead to breakthroughs. I'd like you to take responsibility for collaboration."

"What does that mean?"

"It means taking responsibility for the success of your colleagues, as well as the success of the project."

"How do I do that? I have no authority over my

IMAGINE SOLVING THE MOST COMPLEX PROBLEMS

colleagues."

"You don't need authority. Here's how it works. Think about your underlying assumptions about your colleagues, about me, and about yourself. In particular, consider assumptions that explain why you believe others to be threats. These assumptions are probably not flattering, but your behavior is based upon them. Sometimes these assumptions are revealed in the heat of arguments."[15]

"Okay, I've got a few."

"You might write them down."

"I'll remember them."

"Can you explain the cause-and-effect relationship between your assumptions about your colleagues and your behavior?"

"Sure. I believe Celsius makes bad decisions. I raise issues to prevent his bad decisions from causing failure."

"Good. Let's use the word assume instead of believe, because assumptions are more easily changed than beliefs. Now, think about the assumptions your colleagues may create based upon your behavior. These assumptions are probably not flattering either. Your colleagues' behavior toward you is based upon their assumptions."

"I'm not following you."

"You're very good at finding issues, and you raise them as fast as you find them. Think about how your behavior is received by others. What assumptions could they create about you?"

Aqua thinks for a minute. "I've been told I'm all criticism and no solutions."

"I'll bet that was said in the heat of an argument."

"Just last week."

"Now, for a hard question: Why do you think your

ICEBERG DOWN: BUILDING HIGH-PERFORMANCE TEAMS

raising issues bothers your colleague so much?"

"I have no idea. I can't be responsible for what Celsius is thinking."

"That's why this is a hard question. Think about what Celsius is trying to accomplish. Think about responsibility through his eyes."

After a moment Aqua says, "Maybe he sees my raising issues without offering alternative ideas as a threat."

"That's right. You see his decisions as a threat. He sees your raising issues as a threat. These opposing viewpoints cause us to act as we do. We see threats, and we defend ourselves against those threats, and we do so in the name of responsibility and because we think we are right. What could you do to change Celsius' assumption?"

Aqua thinks for a minute. "Instead of just raising an issue, I could take a few minutes to try to think of a solution to the issue and mention both at the same time."

"How would that help?" Aristotle asks.

"Maybe he would think I'm trying to help him be successful."

"Excellent. A few organizations do what you just described. I know of one that calls it "Plussing an idea." You make an idea better by both raising and resolving an issue."[14]

Plussing, Aqua says to herself.

"What if you can't think of a Plus?" Aristotle asks. "Are there other things you could do when your colleagues make a suggestion that doesn't make sense to you?"

"I could ask others if they have ideas that might resolve the issue."

"Anything else?"

"I could ask questions to try to find out why he thinks

his idea is a good one."

"Very good. Are you willing to give collaborative responsibility a try?"

"I don't know. What are the chances it will work?"

"Behavior is not governed by physics, so it doesn't work all the time, particularly when there's a history of defensive behavior. But collaborative behavior can be contagious. Besides, what do you have to lose?"

"My sanity." Aqua thinks for a moment. "If this collaborative responsibility doesn't work, can I take a leave of absence?"

"Fair enough."

"Okay, I'll try it."

Chapter 25

A New Approach

Aqua enters the conference room that morning with an updated customer document. Celsius, Nitro and Frostbite are already in the room, looking at the gap diagram.

"I think we should pursue a layer of solid ice using fresh water," Celsius says.

"I agree," Nitro says. "It's our best chance."

"Frostbite," Celsius says. "How thick does a solid layer of ice need to be if we make it from fresh water?"

"I'd have to do some experiments."

Celsius glances at Aqua. She is tempted to say it's a bad idea because the layer of ice will melt under the warmer lake water, but she remembers Aristotle's advice. She can't think of a plus, so she decides to ask for ideas.

"I called Meredith," Aqua announces. "I asked her the questions we discussed yesterday. She said her capacity is six billion gallons per month, and she can take up to six billion gallons starting in September. She can increase capacity starting in March. Also, she'll take the water anytime during the month."

Aqua points to the customer wall chart. "Meredith gave me this advice. She wants one thing by October. She wants liquid water in the Middle East. She doesn't care about all the other stuff we do, like building lakes and hiring whales, as long as she receives fresh water in the Middle East in October. She suggested we think out of the box, the box being lakes of fresh water melted on the top of an iceberg. Any ideas?"

Aqua sits down on the other side of the table.

"I've got a crazy idea," Nitro says. "We could wrap a plastic bag around an iceberg and tow it to the Middle East. The warm water up north would melt it."

"We might want to consider small icebergs if we're going to wrap them in plastic," Celsius laughs. "They'd melt faster."

"We can always break icebergs into small pieces," Nitro says.

Aqua jumps up. *"I've got a Plus,"* she says to herself.

"I think you're on to something. Let's take advantage of the fact that icebergs have weak tensile strength. What if we were to break icebergs into small pieces and lift them into tankers? Then we just have to make sure the ice melts by the time it arrives in the Middle East."

"I like that," Celsius says. "Frostbite, what will it take to melt a tanker full of ice?"

"It's not trivial. A lot of energy is required to melt ice. We would have to work closely with Hydro for Humanity."

"Nitro," Celsius says, "how hard is it to break icebergs into small pieces of ice?"

"I can break icebergs into any size you want. And I

know of companies in Penguin City that make grabbing implements to pick ice out of the water and load it into tankers."

"Can you call them?" Aqua says. "When you find out, let us all know. Then we'll call Aristotle."

"I think this solution just might work." Celsius says.

"I'm going to capture these ideas," Aqua says as she draws a new table.

****

Three hours later, the penguins reconvene in the conference room.

"I talked to two companies," Nitro says. "Both can modify grabbing implements they already have and install them on boats. One can do it in two weeks, and the other in four weeks. The weight limit will probably be around 10,000 pounds, which is only about five cubic yards, so we'll have to break the iceberg into very small pieces."

"Let's call Aristotle," Aqua says. She calls him, puts him on speaker, and explains the plan.

"Very good," Aristotle says. "This idea is the type of out-of-the-box thinking we need. Here's what I'd like you to do: Please prepare a one-page proposal."

"What information should be in it?" Aqua asks.

"First, you need a couple of bullets on the background and current situation. You need to state your objectives. Then you need a description of the proposal and alternatives for implementation."

"Give me a second," Aqua says. "I'm writing this down. Okay, what else?"

"Most important, you need to identify issues and

assumptions."

"I've got background, current situation, objectives, proposal description, alternatives, and issues and assumptions. Is that everything?"

"Yes. Now let me tell you what you don't need. You don't need to restate customer requirements because they are already on the wall. You don't need to mention anything about making a lake of fresh water on icebergs because that information is already on the wall. You don't need to list the other ideas you considered because they are also on the wall."

"Anything else?"

"No, that's it. I'll meet you in the conference room at one o'clock tomorrow. Please don't tell Meredith until I have a chance to review the plan."

Chapter 26

Those Prickly Issues

"How is Dr. Bond?" Celsius asks.

Aristotle takes a deep breath. "Not good. I found out he's suffering from Mad Emperor's Disease."

"Mad Emperor's Disease?" Celsius and Nitro say together.

"I talked to Dr. Sigmund Penguin, the head of the Psychology Department at Penguin University. He said Dr. Bond is incapable of effective self-reflection. He interprets all results and feedback as evidence that supports his beliefs."

"Will he recover?" Aqua asks.

"Yes. Dr. Sigmund Penguin expects a full recovery."

"That's good," Aqua says.

"Okay," Aristotle says. "Let's see what you have."

"The beauty of this plan," Aqua says, "is that we can start loading tankers as soon as we move the iceberg to a safe distance north of the Ross Ice Shelf. Nitro can cut and detonate ice to any size we need. Frostbite will work with Hydro for Humanity to make sure the ice melts en route to the Middle East."

Proposal: Break iceberg into Small Pieces and Lift into Tankers. Ice melts en route to Middle East.

Background / Current Situation:
1. Humans are desperate for fresh water.
2. Hydro for Humanity has requested large volumes of fresh water (see Customer document).

Objectives:
1. Find a safe and reliable way to harvest fresh water from icebergs.
2. Meet Hydro for Humanity schedule requirements: fresh water in the Middle East starting in October.

Proposal description:
1. Whales push iceberg 400 miles north.
2. Break iceberg into small pieces: <10,000 pounds each.
3. Grabbers on boats pick ice from sea and load into tankers.
4. Ice melts en route to customers.

Alternatives for Implementation:
1. Company A can deliver grabbers on boats in 2 weeks.
2. Company B (larger) can deliver in 4 weeks.

Issues and assumptions:
1. Cost and speed of grabber boats.
2. How to melt ice en route.
3. Ensure ice is loaded into tankers safely.
4. Ensure small icebergs don't damage tankers and stay out of shipping lanes.

Implementation schedule:
1. Implement proposal steps 1-3 by August 31.
2. Begin loading tankers – September 1.
3. Tankers arrive in the Middle East with melted water October 1.

Figure 26-1

Aristotle reads the document from top to bottom.

"Well done. I particularly like the issues and assumptions. The first two deal with reliable delivery and the last two deal with safety. Which do you think will be the hardest to overcome?"

"I'd suggest we move forward with both companies that make grabber instruments," Nitro says. "We'll have to determine how fast we can load the tankers and how many grabbers we need."

"How about melting the ice?" Aristotle says.

"A lot of energy is required to melt ice," Frostbite says. "We'll have to work with Hydro for Humanity to see what the options are. I don't have an answer yet."

"I didn't expect you to know at this point. That's why it's an issue."

"We'll also have to work closely with Hydro for Humanity to ensure ice is loaded safely into tankers," Aqua says.

"How about the last issue?" Aristotle asks. "How can we keep small icebergs away from tankers and shipping lanes?"

"I think that's the hardest one," Aqua says. "We're going to need lots of whales and penguins. We may need to quarantine the area. No ships allowed except tankers."

Aristotle asks, "How close are the shipping lanes to your pickup point?"

"I have a map," Nitro says. "Traffic is light just north of the Ross Ice Shelf."

"You're right. It's not a busy area as shipping lanes go, but scientists, cruise ships, and tourists travel fairly regularly from New Zealand down to the Ross Ice Shelf."

Aristotle walks to the front of the room. "This is good,

out-of-the-box thinking, but serious issues have to be resolved for this plan to succeed, particularly safety. I'd like you to think about whether it makes sense to try to resolve these issues or brainstorm other ideas."

Aqua points to the Learn-Ideas-Test-Decide chart. "This is a potentially viable solution. Shouldn't we at least test it with Meredith? Test is the next step."

"What do the rest of you think?" Aristotle asks.

"I think we should test it with Meredith and Dalton immediately," Celsius says.

Nitro nods in agreement.

"Test is the next step," Aristotle says. "But that doesn't mean every idea is tested with a customer. This is a creative idea, but it has serious issues. I'd like you to think about it some more."

"You do realize there is little time," Celsius says.

"Trust me when I say I do."

"I don't want to give up on this idea," Aqua says. "We can meet Meredith's needs."

Frostbite opens his mouth as if to talk, but says nothing.

"Frostbite," Aristotle says. "Do you want to say something?"

"Just yawning."

"You might consider going back to the Learn step," Aristotle says. "Maybe a similar problem has been solved in another industry. You might do some research."

Aristotle leaves.

Celsius turns to his colleagues. "Aristotle is the opposite of Dr. Bond. He can't make a decision."

"Now is the time for action," Aqua says. "We have a great plan."

After a moment, Aqua says, "I think I know what is going on here." She quickly leaves.

Aqua marches through the lobby to Aristotle's office. His door is open, but the office is empty. A sign on his desk says he is in the Sculpture Lab.

Aqua walks outside and around the greenhouse. She enters the lab. Ice sculptures adorn shelves near the entrance. Long benches are lined with ice blocks. Dozens of saws, saw blades, grinders, and drills of all shapes and sizes hang on the wall. Aristotle is cutting some detail on a statue with a portable grinder.

Aqua enters. Aristotle sees her and turns off the grinder.

"Do you sculpt?" Aristotle asks.

"Not since college."

"It's my hobby. I've done it since I was a kid. I do it to relax. You're welcome to use this lab anytime."

"I know. I mean, thank you."

Aristotle points to the shelf, "You're welcome to any of those sculptures."

Aqua glances at the shelf containing ice sculptures of penguins, whales, humans, and many fish. She picks up a small statue of a baby penguin and inspects the fine detail.

"What a week," Aqua says. "I can't believe Dr. Bond was arrested. Do you think you'll be called to testify at the trial?"

"It's possible."

"Have you talked to a lawyer?"

"No."

After a minute, Aristotle asks, "Can I ask what you are concerned about?"

"It occurred to me that with Dr. Bond in so much

trouble, we really can't afford to take any risks."

"Do you think I didn't approve your proposal because Dr. Bond was arrested?"

Aqua looks up. Her expression answers his question.

"First of all, thank you for telling me. I appreciate it. Do you mind if I tell the others what you told me?"

"Not at all."

Chapter 27

Collaborative Responsibility

"Thank you for joining me on such short notice," Aristotle says. "Aqua shared a concern with me that I'd like you all to be aware of."

"Aqua, could you share your concern?"

"I asked Aristotle if he was being overly cautious because Dr. Bond was arrested."

"I think you meant that if Dr. Bond had not been arrested, I would have approved your proposal. And by the way, I want to thank you for trusting me enough to tell me."

Aristotle looks at each penguin. "Aqua helped me realize something. I've been telling all of you to admit mistakes, but I haven't been admitting my own mistakes."

Aqua, Celsius, Nitro and Frostbite exchange glances.

"I violated one of my own rules: I made assumptions and didn't test them.[15] I assumed Dr. Bond, being a penguin, was an innocent victim of corrupt humans and he could be reformed. Actually, I assumed that I could reform him. I've read lots of books about corrupt humans. I fell into the age-old trap of blaming individuals who are not like me. So I offered to do a Learning-to-Succeed exercise. Then I believed everything Dr. Bond said and invited him to tell you what he learned."

Aristotle draws.

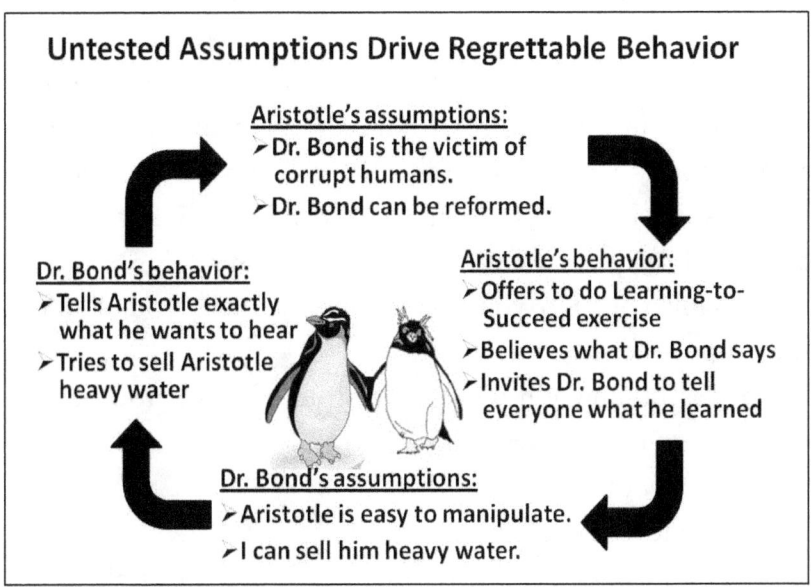

Figure 27-1

"He played me like a harp. He assumed I was easy to manipulate and that he could sell me heavy water. So he told me exactly what I wanted to hear, which reinforced my assumption that he was a victim of corrupt humans and that I could reform him. I even believed him when he said he changed his name back to Henry Penguin."

"What should you have done?" Aqua asks.

"I should have tested my assumption before offering to do a Learning-to-Succeed exercise. I could easily have found out he had taken a new job and was trying to sell heavy water. Then I wouldn't have offered to do the Learning-to-Succeed exercise with him."

Aristotle looks at each employee.

"I want each of you to be open and honest about this proposal. I'd like to start with Frostbite because I don't remember him saying anything earlier."

"Me?" Frostbite says. He takes a deep breath. "I'm worried. What if a storm hits like the one that hit Atlantis and we have dozens of tiny icebergs in the pickup area? We'll never find them. We'll never keep them away from ships. Storms will happen, and we will have an accident with a ship. It's just a matter of time. Look, I know we need a solution, but we can't risk sinking ships."

"Thank you. Do you mind telling us why you didn't speak up earlier?"

"I was hoping you would have told us it was too risky because you're the boss."

"But why didn't you speak up?"

Frostbite is silent.

"Frostbite has a point," Aqua says. "If you think this proposal is too risky, why don't you tell us, so we can move on to other ideas. We're wasting time."

"I don't think we're wasting time. We're building a high-performance team, so this time is well spent. We are going to face hard problems, problems that can only be solved by a high-performance team. I could make every decision, and we could start implementation, but I'm not smart enough to foresee all the downstream problems. None of us is, by ourselves."

Aristotle looks at Frostbite. "Would you like to tell me your concerns in private?"

Frostbite looks down. "I didn't want to disagree with

IMAGINE SOLVING THE MOST COMPLEX PROBLEMS

Aqua because she has been so good to me. She hired me at Atlantis right out of college." He pauses and looks up. "I'm the junior guy, and I didn't want to burn bridges."

"So you didn't say anything because you assumed Aqua would hold it against you and she's your best friend at work?"

"She's my only friend at work."

"Why do you say that?" Aristotle asks.

"It's no secret that Aqua and Celsius don't get along. Nitro always sides with Celsius, and I guess I'm supposed to always side with Aqua."

"Thank you for putting that issue out there. You're right. It's no secret. We'll discuss Aqua and Celsius in a minute."

Aqua groans.

Aristotle looks at each individual. "What is absolutely necessary for sensitive issues to be raised?"

"Trust," Aqua answers. "Trust that others won't hold your opinion against you."

Aristotle addresses the team. "Frostbite assumes he can't disagree with Aqua on something she is passionate about for fear of burning a bridge. He keeps quiet in order to preserve his relationship with Aqua. Aqua assumes Frostbite agrees with her, and since Frostbite is smart, she assumes she must be right. She defends her ideas even more strongly, which reinforces Frostbite's assumption that he had better not disagree with her. Aqua was so sure she was right, she assumed I became overly risk-averse because Dr. Bond was arrested. I doubt Aqua would have formed that opinion if Frostbite had spoken up."

"I had no idea how Frostbite felt," Aqua says.

Aristotle looks at Celsius and Nitro. "Let me ask you a

question. Were Aqua and Frostbite being responsible?"

"Yes," Celsius says. "Aqua was taking responsibility for solving the problem."

"Frostbite was taking responsibility for maintaining his relationship with Aqua," Nitro says.

"Right. They were both being responsible but in a defensive way, not in a collaborative way."

Aristotle draws.[15]

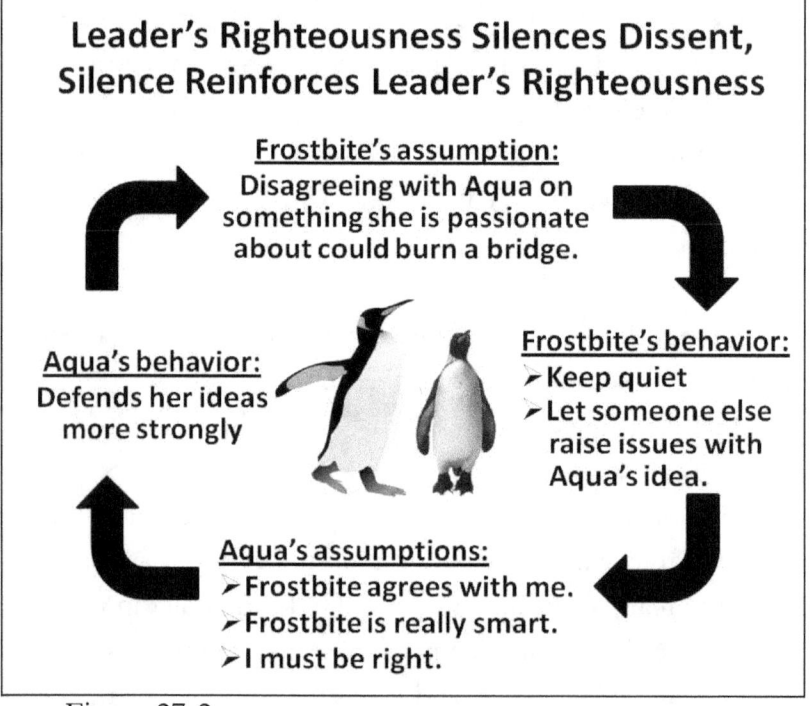

Figure 27-2

Aqua turns to Frostbite. "I'm sorry."

Aristotle adds, "Imagine what happens when executives are afraid to raise important issues with a CEO, and as a result, the CEO takes a bad plan to the Board of Directors and investors."

"The company fails," Aqua says.

IMAGINE SOLVING THE MOST COMPLEX PROBLEMS

"It happens all the time," Aristotle says.

"It happened at Atlantis," Celsius says. "I submitted a plan to Dr. Bond describing how ten Atlantis-like icebergs would be built in one year. I knew the plan wouldn't work. I did it because I was afraid to tell Dr. Bond I didn't know how to do it. He had already announced the project would succeed. I was not going to tell him the plan wasn't possible. He didn't tolerate excuses."

Aqua looks at Aristotle. "Can you explain how all these business experts could hail Dr. Bond as a great leader? He was guessing."

"I can't speak for anyone who said Dr. Bond was a great leader. But Atlantis' experience demonstrates that when leaders create a culture that doesn't allow problems, mistakes or excuses, the probability of success decreases."

Aristotle looks at Aqua and Frostbite, "What could you two do to take responsibility for being collaborative?"

"I could ask Frostbite what he thinks," Aqua says.

"I'm curious. Why didn't you?"

"It never occurred to me. I'm used to Frostbite agreeing with me, and he's right about me and Celsius. I would have felt betrayed if Frostbite had agreed with Celsius and not with me."

Aqua turns to Frostbite. "From now on, I'll ask you for your ideas and not worry about who you agree with."

"Frostbite, what could you have done?" Aristotle asks.

"I could have approached Aqua when she was alone and told her I didn't think her idea would work and why."

"Very good. As Aqua proactively asks Frostbite for issues and ideas, he should begin to assume he can raise any issue or idea without fear of reprisal. As Frostbite proactively raises ideas and issues, Aqua should begin to assume she can count on him to speak up when he sees issues or has ideas. This type of interaction is collaborative responsibility."

Aristotle turns to the whole group. "A few days ago I asked Aqua to take responsibility for collaboration. Aqua, can you share what you did?"

"You explained that if we're spending our time behaving defensively, we aren't likely to find the breakthroughs we need. You asked me to do two things. First, you asked me to identify the underlying assumptions that drive my behavior. Second, you asked me to think about how my behavior affects my colleagues, particularly colleagues I consider threats."

Aqua looks at Celsius. "I was raising issues because I assumed a colleague made uninformed decisions, and unless I raised issues, his decisions would cause failure."

"I'll bet I'm that colleague," Celsius says.

"To be honest, yes, you are. I rationalized that the right thing to do was to raise issues even when it sounded like criticism. The real breakthrough came when I realized my behavior could be viewed as being obstinate, raising issues rather than just doing what I was asked."

"Thank you, Aqua," Aristotle says. "Because our assumptions are often not flattering, we don't mention them for fear of making the situation worse."

"Do you want to hear my side?" Celsius asks.

"I do," Aristotle says. "Aqua, are you willing to hear Celsius' side?"

"Yes."

"I assumed one of my colleagues was undependable because she was criticizing decisions instead of doing what she was asked when I was counting on her. Because I assumed she was undependable, I constantly reminded her to do what she was asked to do."

Aristotle turns to Aqua. "What did you assume about Celsius when he reminded you to do what you were asked?"

"Reminding me to do what I was asked reinforced my assumption that he made bad decisions."

Aristotle looks at Nitro and Frostbite. "Were they being responsible?"

"Celsius was taking responsibility for getting things done," Nitro says.

"Aqua was taking responsibility for preventing failure," Frostbite says.

"Did they ever mention their frustration?"

Frostbite and Nitro nod yes.

"But not to each other. This is a perfect example of how, in the name of responsibility, we achieve something that is much different from what we want."

Aristotle draws.[15]

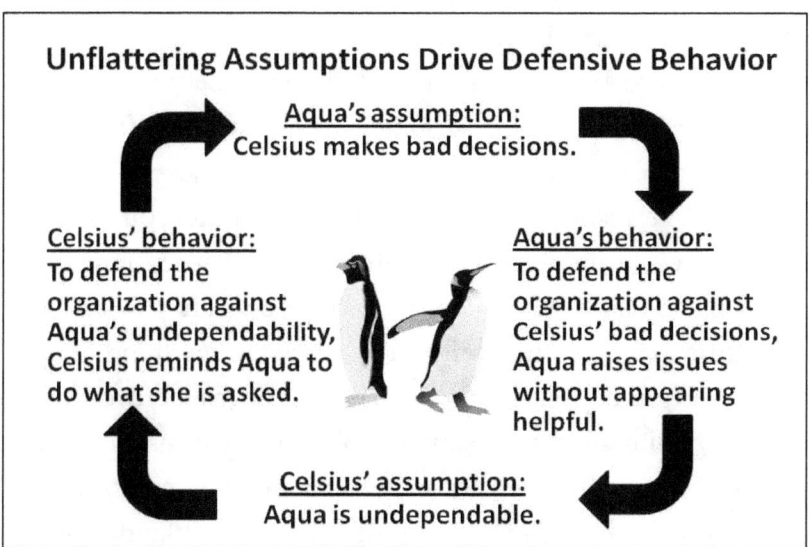

Figure 27-3

"We assume we have to defend ourselves against threats, but our defensive behavior causes others to see us as threats. Worse, work becomes miserable and the team becomes paralyzed. This type of behavior is defensive responsibility. The only way to break the cycle is to change behavior. Then, over time, assumptions will most likely change. Collaborative behavior can be contagious."

"The last thing I want be seen as is undependable," Aqua says.

"The last thing I want to be known for is bad decisions," Celsius says.

"Aqua, can you tell us what you decided to do to break the cycle and take responsibility for collaboration?"

"I did three things. First, I decided to ask questions to find out why my colleagues think their ideas are good. Second, I decided to ask others for ideas. Third, I decided to try to think of ways to potentially resolve the issues that I see with their ideas. That way my colleagues would perceive me as building upon their ideas and assume I'm trying to help them be successful."

"The third behavior is called 'Plussing', because she is improving ideas. Aqua is taking responsibility for the success of her colleagues and the project. That's collaborative responsibility. Celsius, what could you do to break the cycle and take responsibility for collaboration?"

"I could ask Aqua what issues she sees." He pauses. "I should probably ask her before I've made up my mind."

"Very good. Asking for issues and ideas before you make up your mind is essential. Colleagues can usually tell if you're asking for their ideas before drawing conclusions or if you have already made up your mind and want confirmation. If colleagues assume you want confirmation, they can withhold ideas and information to avoid burning bridges, as Frostbite did, or speak up and risk being seen as undependable, as Aqua did. Both of these cycles of defensive behavior decrease the probability of success."

"I have something to get off my chest," Celsius says slowly. "The idea to make a layer of ice with heavy water and sawdust was not mine. It was Dr. Bond's. I've been talking to Dr. Bond regularly since I joined here. He's been telling me what to do."

"Thank you for telling us," Aristotle says. "I'm curious why you acted that way. You can tell me alone later, if you prefer or not at all."

"I can tell everyone why. There are two reasons. First, Dr. Bond was the world-renowned expert. Second, he made me a vice president. My parents and wife were so proud. I believed I owed Dr. Bond my loyalty. Now I realize he has an addiction. At Atlantis, all he had to do was drain the lake, but instead he kept filling it because the bigger the lake became, the more money and fame he received."

"Thank you. It's important that teams don't harbor secrets. Is there anything else anyone would like to mention?"

"Yes," Aqua says. "Some of you know I've been reluctant to work on icebergs. The reason is: running around Atlantis screaming, 'Iceberg Down,' just before the iceberg broke was the worst experience of my life. I don't ever want to go through that again."

"Thank you. Are there other issues anyone would like to raise?"

"Yes," Nitro says. "What happens if we can't find a safe and reliable solution? Will we lose our jobs?"

"No, you will not lose your jobs. We need four more penguins on the glacier side of the business, but those jobs may not be as interesting as you would like."

"What if a new job doesn't require expertise in explosives or cutting? That's pretty much all I do."

"If that were to happen, we will retrain you."

"Thanks. I was worried."

"I have a question for you," Aristotle says. "Did you support implementation of the proposal to build a lakebed from ice made with heavy water and sawdust and the proposal to break the iceberg into small pieces because you thought they were the right things to do or because you were worried about your job?"

Nitro's eyes widen.

"You can tell me alone later."

"I'll tell everyone. I was worried about my job. To be honest, I haven't paid much attention to the ideas. I always let Celsius worry about that. Celsius has been good to me so I side with him. But like Frostbite, I'm tired of the feud between Aqua and Celsius. Also, I've been laid off and out of work. It's no fun. So, I've been looking for ways to keep busy doing what I do well, and I don't complain."

"That's my fault," Aristotle says. "I've been meaning to talk with each of you about what you think and what you're worried about, but I haven't found the time because I've been traveling so much. I could have relieved Nitro's fears of losing his job."

Aristotle turns to Nitro. "I am sorry."

Aristotle turns to Celsius, Aqua and Frostbite. "Was Nitro being responsible?"

"Yes," Celsius says. "He was taking responsibility for keeping his job.

IMAGINE SOLVING THE MOST COMPLEX PROBLEMS

Aristotle draws another chart.[15]

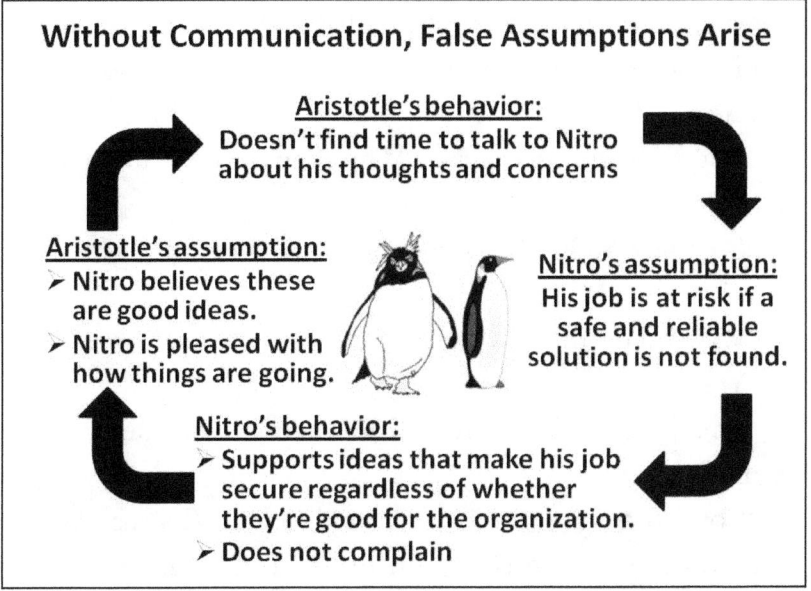

Figure 27-4

"Because I didn't talk to Nitro, he assumed his job was in danger. He supported ideas he thought would make his job secure regardless of whether they were good for the organization, and he didn't complain. I assumed Nitro thought the ideas were good and that he was pleased with how things are going. I didn't see an urgent need to meet with him. As a result, Nitro was unnecessarily stressed, and we lost the benefit of Nitro's ideas and insights. Hopefully he will change his assumption and his behavior."

"I thought about stopping by your office, but I figured you were too busy."

"Assuming leaders are too busy is common, particularly when an organization has lots of problems. Leaders feel responsible for fixing problems, so they spend all their time working on the problems. As a result, they don't find time to talk to employees. Employees assume the worst and behave in ways they assume will protect their jobs. Behavior becomes defensive, collaboration suffers, the situation deteriorates, and the worst-case assumptions become true."

Aristotle turns to Nitro. "What can you do to break this cycle?"

"I could study the ideas and tell everyone what I think."

"Will you do that?"

"Yes."

"Thank you. I look forward to hearing your ideas and insights."

"Collaborative behavior is complicated," Celsius says. "Can you leave these charts on the wall? I want to study them."

"Absolutely." Aristotle smiles because Celsius finally sees value in wall charts. "Changing from defensive behavior to collaborative behavior requires work. But once we learn to change our behavior, we find that we are far more powerful than we thought. Remember, our most important assumptions are about each other."

Aristotle looks at each one of the penguins. "I hope you all understand the difference between defensive responsibility and collaborative responsibility. Remember, taking responsibility for collaboration leads to breakthroughs."

"I have a question," Frostbite says. "These wall charts work when we're all in the same room. But what if the audience is in Penguin City or Christchurch? A wall chart wouldn't work."

"After the prime minister called Monday, I sent her a one-page document clearly describing the background,

IMAGINE SOLVING THE MOST COMPLEX PROBLEMS

current situation, goals, analysis including a picture of the gap diagram, alternatives, and next steps. She called back because she thought I had told her something different over the phone. Since she was including my comments in a report to the UN, she was appreciative of the written document because she did not want her report to the UN to be inaccurate."

"Why didn't you write her an e-mail or send a few slides?" Celsius asks.

"When topics are complex, e-mails can be confusing. Although slides are easy to prepare, I have a hard time following slides because I can't remember what was on the previous slides. With practice, I've learned to write concise one-page documents so it's easy for the reader to connect the dots between a problem or opportunity, analysis, alternatives, and implementation."

"I was taught to write A3s in a Lean Production course," Celsius says. "I was told to use eleven-inch-by-seventeen-inch paper, two columns, and landscape orientation. Is that what you mean?"

"The size of the paper and orientation of the document don't matter. The goal is to make the one-page document clear and concise so the audience can understand it quickly. I break topics into small pieces. It's easier to understand two letter-size documents than one eleven-inch-by-seventeen-inch document."

"What content goes in one-page documents?" Frostbite asks.

"The content is similar to wall charts."

"Are you saying one-page documents improve understanding and credibility?" Frostbite asks.

"Yes, and they promote problem solving. I wish more

executives and government leaders would use one-page documents. A lot of misunderstandings could be avoided."

Aristotle walks to the front of the room. "Although we haven't tested the proposal to break icebergs into small pieces, load the pieces into tankers, and melt en route, it's time to formally decide whether we're going to try to resolve the issues associated with this proposal or look for other ideas. I'd like to hear everyone's opinion."

Frostbite looks at his colleagues. "Because of the safety issue, I think we should look for other ideas."

Nitro adds: "I'm also worried about speed. Picking ice out of the ocean could be very slow. I think we should look for other ideas."

"Can we come back to this idea if we can't find anything better?" Celsius asks.

"Absolutely," Aristotle says. "Who knows? You might figure out how to resolve the issues."

"Okay. Then I support looking for other ideas."

"I agree," Aqua says softly. "It's too dangerous."

Aristotle smiles. "It's decided. We look for other ideas."

Part IV Summary

Aristotle had to find a way to turn defensive behavior into collaborative behavior. But first, he had to bring secrets out into the open.

He started by explaining to Aqua that high-performance teams are created when someone steps up and figures out how to change his or her behavior in such a way that others respond differently.

Then, Aristotle explained that there are two types of responsibility: defensive and collaborative. Defensive responsibility may stop threats, but it is not likely to lead to breakthroughs. Collaborative responsibility means taking responsibility for colleagues' success and the project's success.

Aristotle asked Aqua to identify the underlying assumptions that drove her behavior and to think about how her behavior could affect her colleagues, particularly colleagues she considered threats.

The following cycles of reinforcing defensive behavior

were revealed.

	Assumption and Behavior	Response Assumption and Behavior
1	Aristotle assumed: • Dr. Bond was an innocent victim of corrupt humans. • He could reform Dr. Bond. Aristotle conducted a Learning-to-Succeed exercise and believed what Dr. Bond said.	Dr. Bond assumed: • Aristotle was easy to manipulate • Aristotle would buy heavy water from him. Dr. Bond told Aristotle exactly what he wanted to hear, which reinforced Aristotle's assumption that he could reform Dr. Bond.
2	Frostbite assumed that disagreeing with Aqua on something she was passionate about could burn a bridge, so he kept his concerns to himself.	Because Frostbite did not raise his concern, Aqua assumed Frostbite agreed with her, so she defended her ideas more strongly.
3	Aqua assumed Celsius makes bad decisions, so she raised issues even when doing so sounded critical.	Because Aqua raised issues instead of just doing what she was asked, Celsius assumed Aqua was undependable, so he constantly reminded her to do what she was asked.
4	Nitro assumed his job was at risk, so he: • Supported ideas he thought would make his job secure regardless of whether they were good ideas. • Did not complain.	Aristotle assumed Nitro thought the ideas were good, and that he was pleased with how things were going, so Aristotle assumed there was no urgent need to meet with Nitro.

Figure IV–1

The following was also revealed.
1. In the name of responsibility, Aqua and Celsius achieved a much different outcome than they wanted. Aqua did not want to be known for being undependable. Celsius did not want to be known for making bad decisions.
2. Aqua admitted she would have felt betrayed if Frostbite had agreed with Celsius and disagreed with her.
3. Celsius admitted he submitted a plan to Dr. Bond describing how ten Atlantis-like icebergs would be built in one year even though he knew it wouldn't work because he was afraid to admit he didn't know how to do it. Aristotle pointed out that when leaders create a culture that doesn't allow problems, mistakes or excuses, the probability of success decreases.
4. Celsius admitted the layer of heavy ice with sawdust was Dr. Bond's idea, and that he had been talking to Dr. Bond regularly. He said he remained loyal to Dr. Bond because Dr. Bond was a world-renowned expert, and because he promoted Celsius to vice president.
5. Aqua shared that she was reluctant to work on icebergs because running around Atlantis screaming "Iceberg Down" just before the iceberg broke was the worst experience of her life, and she doesn't ever want to do that again.

Aristotle asked the penguins what they could do to break the cycle of defensive behavior. The following chart shows what they agreed to do and the assumptions they hope will result. The chart also shows Aristotle's collaborative behavior and the assumptions he hopes will result.

	Collaborative Behavior	Hoped for Assumption
1	Aqua agreed to: • Inquire to find out why colleagues think their ideas are good. • Ask for ideas. • Try to resolve the issues with colleagues' ideas.	• Aqua is trying to help colleagues and the project be successful. • Aqua is dependable.
2	Aqua agreed to ask Frostbite what he thinks without worrying about who he agrees with.	Frostbite can disagree with Aqua without fear of burning a bridge.
3	Frostbite agreed to raise issues and suggest ideas.	Frostbite can be counted on to say what he thinks.
4	Nitro agreed to study ideas and tell others what he really thinks	Nitro can be counted on to raise issues and suggest ideas.
5	Celsius agreed to ask Aqua what her issues and ideas are before making up his mind.	• Celsius wants to understand issues and prevent failure. • Celsius makes good decisions.
6	Aristotle thanked Aqua twice for telling him she thought he was being more risk-averse because Dr. Bond was arrested, once privately and again in front of the entire group.	It is safe to approach Aristotle with any issue or idea, no matter how sensitive or threatening.
7	Aristotle apologized to Nitro for not finding time to meet.	Aristotle takes responsibility for problems. He doesn't blame others.

Figure IV–2

IMAGINE SOLVING THE MOST COMPLEX PROBLEMS

After the discussion about collaborative behavior, Aristotle announced that he would like to formally decide whether to try to resolve the issues associated with the proposal to break icebergs into small pieces, load the pieces into tankers, and melt en route, or look for other ideas.

All four penguins supported looking for other ideas.

Now we'll see if there is enough commitment to find a solution in time to save the humans.

Part V: Collaborating Team

Chapter 28

Research

It's after five o'clock, and most penguins have gone home. Aqua walks down to the Sculpture Lab. It's locked and the lights are off. She swipes her badge in the electronic reader, waits for the door latch to open, and enters the dark room.

She turns on the light and picks up a small block of ice. *I used to be pretty good at this.* Feeling the cold sink into her fin, she walks over to a saw and cuts off a few pieces of ice. She then uses a grinder to make a rough shape of a penguin's head. She thinks about what Aristotle said about Plussing. *We need a plus that resolves the issue of loose iceberg remnants getting in the way of ships.*

"Wait a minute," she says out loud. "We can't be the first ones who've tried to sell ice. What did humans do before refrigerators?"

She runs upstairs, turns on her computer, and searches the history of the ice business in America.

The American ice industry started around Boston in the early

IMAGINE SOLVING THE MOST COMPLEX PROBLEMS

1800s and grew rapidly. People used ice to keep food cold in the summer and to make ice cream. Ice from American rivers and lakes was stored in insulated icehouses and shipped as far away as India. In 1879 eight million tons of ice were harvested. That's almost two billion gallons! They did all this with horse-drawn saws and steam-driven conveyers[16]

"That's it!" she shouts. *We'll carve the iceberg into blocks of ice and use a conveyer to load the ice blocks into the tankers. If two billion gallons can be harvested with horses and steam-engines, we should be able to do much better with today's technology. And we won't have a minefield of tiny icebergs to worry about.*

Aqua jumps up and runs back to the lobby. Aristotle's office is closed. He has gone home. *He's going to want a one-page proposal.* She goes to work.

****

Aqua arrives early Thursday morning in time to make a few modifications to her proposal and attach it to the wall before anyone else arrives.

She settles into a chair as Celsius, Nitro and Frostbite enter.

"Good morning," Aqua says.

"You look tired," Frostbite says.

"I didn't sleep much."

"Do we have a new proposal?" Celsius says as he walks over to the wall and reads the document. Frostbite and Nitro read the proposal too.

"Of course," Frostbite says. "Humans had a thriving ice business before refrigerators. That's how they kept food cold in the summer."

"And they made ice cream," Aqua adds.

"I like it," Celsius says. "I like it a lot."

PROPOSAL: Cut Small blocks of Ice off of Iceberg and Convey into Tankers. Ice melts en route to Customers.

Background:
1. Humans are desperate for freshwater.
2. Hydro for Humanity has requested large volumes of fresh water (see Customer document).

Objectives:
1. Find a safe and reliable way to harvest fresh water from icebergs.
2. Meet Hydro for Humanity schedule requirements: fresh water in the Middle East starting in October.

Proposal Description:
1. Whales push icebergs to pick-up zone 400 miles north of Ross Ice Shelf.
2. Build maintenance shed on iceberg fully equipped to build cutting and conveyance equipment.
3. Cut small blocks of ice off icebergs and convey into tankers.
4. Ice melts en route to customers.

Issues and Assumptions:
1. Finding companies that can provide high speed saws and conveyers and meet schedule at reasonable cost.
2. How to melt ice en route.

Implementation Schedule: To be determined

Figure 28-1

"Does anyone know of companies that can make the saws and conveyers we need?" Aqua asks.

"The two companies that make grabbers also make saws and conveyers," Nitro answers.

Aristotle enters. "Good morning."

Celsius points to Aqua's proposal. "Aristotle, take a

look at Aqua's new proposal."

Aristotle reads it top to bottom three times. He nods. "Good. What do the rest of you think?"

"Cutting ice blocks off the iceberg will be faster than picking ice out of the sea," Celsius says. "And we won't have any small icebergs in the water that ships might run into."

"What issues do you see?" Aristotle asks.

"It might be expensive," Celsius says.

Aristotle rubs his chin. "I think this proposal has potential, but I want to do one more exercise before we stop searching for better ideas. I want you each to write an obituary."

"A what?" Aqua asks.

"Many organizations dream up headlines where they are enormously successful. Everybody feels good about the plan, at least for a while. Later they find big problems. I prefer writing obituaries because I want to know what can go wrong. I don't want to make a big mistake because we're excited or in a hurry. Any questions?"

The penguins shake their heads.

Aristotle continues: "I want you to imagine things that could go wrong if we implement this proposal to cut blocks off the iceberg and convey the ice blocks into tankers. Think about things that would be very bad for our company, Hydro for Humanity, and human customers. We'll discuss your obituaries this afternoon at one o'clock."

Chapter 29

Plussing It

"Good afternoon," Aristotle says. "Who wants to start?"

"I'll start," Aqua says.

Penguins, Humans Killed In Tanker Accident
Ten humans were killed when large waves caused tons of ice to shift in tankers being filled by Glacier Fresh Water.
A lawyer for a grieving family member said: "The company was clearly negligent for not planning for the action of waves in the ocean. We've starting a class action law suit. We will seek the maximum award."

"Very good," Aristotle says. "Who's next?"

"I've got one," Nitro says.

Penguins Killed in Ice Saw Accident
Six penguins died when a high-speed saw broke loose and spun into a group of penguins working on an iceberg.
Ice-cutting operations have been suspended indefinitely so a complete investigation can be conducted.

"So far we have a tanker accident and a saw accident," Aristotle says. "Celsius, Frostbite?"

"We did ours together," Celsius says.

"Really?" Aqua says.

Frostbite stands. "Since Celsius tried to solve the problem of icebergs breaking, I thought I should talk to him. I should have talked to him a while ago."

"Show them your causal diagram," Celsius says.

Frostbite attaches his causal diagram to the wall.

"Celsius' Five-Why analysis was a good start, but it doesn't explain why icebergs break. Icebergs break when stress is greater than strength. The tensile strength of ice is its resistance to being pulled apart. Stress consists of all the forces that try to pull the iceberg apart. If the sum of the forces pulling the iceberg apart are greater than the tensile strength, the iceberg breaks."

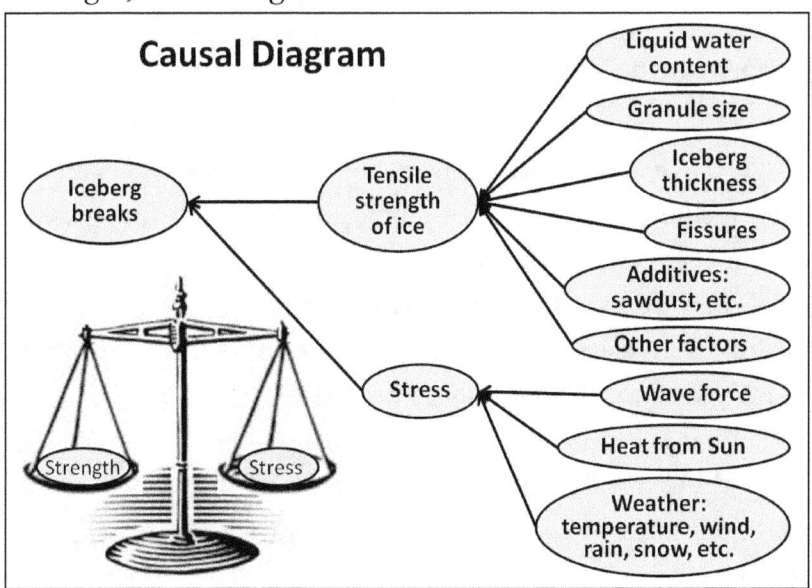

Figure 29-1

Frostbite looks at Celsius. "The causal diagram shows

factors that determine tensile strength and other factors that determine stress. I asked Celsius which ones we can influence or control."

"We selected five very strong, thick icebergs with very small granules," Celsius says. "We can reduce melting by cutting up the iceberg farther south."

"But we can't control wave force, wind or storms," Frostbite says. "Aqua's proposal assumes we can prevent icebergs from breaking. I'm afraid that is a false assumption."

Celsius attaches their obituary to the wall.

> **Ten Die When Iceberg Breaks**
>
> Glacier Fresh Water suffered the same fate as Atlantis when the iceberg it was cutting suddenly broke, sending ten humans to a watery grave. The company also lost all its ice-cutting and conveying equipment.
>
> An analyst said: "Eventually, icebergs break. It's odd that company management didn't consider the danger."

"I knew we couldn't safely and reliably extract water from icebergs," Aqua says, shaking her head. "I knew we couldn't prevent Iceberg Down situations."

"Then we look for other ideas?" Aristotle asks.

Frostbite clears his throat. "I woke early this morning with an idea, but I doubt it will work."

"What is it?" Celsius asks.

"I think it will cost too much."

"Frostbite, we're desperate," Aqua says. "Please tell us your idea."

"I wrote up a one-page document and made copies," Frostbite says as he passes out copies and waits for everyone to read.

IMAGINE SOLVING THE MOST COMPLEX PROBLEMS

PROPOSAL: Cut small blocks off of iceberg and convey into tankers. Ice melts en route to customers.

Background / Current Situation:

1. Cutting small blocks of ice off iceberg and conveying into tankers has potential to meet Hydro for Humanity's requirements.
2. We should assume icebergs will break eventually.

Goal:

Find a way to safely and reliably cut small blocks off of iceberg and convey into tankers.

Evaluation of Alternatives

Alternative	Safety	Reliability	Cost	Schedule
1. Saws and conveyers are secured to iceberg.	If iceberg breaks or storm hits, penguins and humans could be killed or injured.	If iceberg breaks or storm hits, equipment may be damaged, disrupting supply.	Less	Don't know
2. Saws and conveyers are secured to barges docked between iceberg and tankers.	If iceberg breaks or storm hits, barges are undocked. Penguins and humans are safe on barges.	If iceberg breaks or storm hits, equipment is safe on barges.	More	Don't know

Recommendation:

Saws and conveyers secured to barges docked between iceberg and tanker.

Figure 29-2

"Saws and conveyers attached to a barge," Celsius says. "It's a lot safer because if the iceberg breaks no one would be hurt."

"And we don't lose all the equipment," Aqua adds. "If a storm hits, we just undock the barge and wait for the storm to pass."

Securing the equipment to a barge will be easier than securing it to an iceberg," Nitro says. "The barge won't melt."

Aristotle smiles. "I think this plan may have just solved our biggest problem."

"Really?" Frostbite says. "You don't think it will cost too much?"

"Have you thought about how many barges we need?" Aristotle asks.

"I prepared a spreadsheet with three scenarios." Frostbite hands out copies of the spreadsheet as he talks. "The estimate is rough, but it provides ideas for how we might do it."

"Let's start testing this idea," Aristotle says. "We need ballpark quotes on barges, saws, and conveyers. Who can get that?"

"I'm on it," Nitro says. "Frostbite, can you join me?"

"You bet," Frostbite says.

"Call us as soon as you learn something," Aristotle says.

****

"We received a rough quote," Nitro says. "At a capacity of six billion gallons per month, we'll need to load about 120 tankers. We can lease all the barges, saws, and conveyers for $25,000 a month. Or we can purchase everything for $1.5 million. Here's the equipment cost per month if we lease." Nitro hands a spreadsheet to Aristotle.

"Great work," Aristotle says. He creates a table.

Financial Analysis

($000)	Aug	Sept	Oct	Nov	Dec	Jan.	Feb.
Revenue	0	5	40	80	120	120	120
Cost	20	20	50	80	100	100	100
Net cash flow	(20)	(15)	(10)	0	20	20	20
Cumulative cash flow	(20)	(35)	(45)	(45)	(25)	(5)	15

Figure 29-3

"Net cash flow breaks even in November. Cumulative cash flow turns positive in February. We'll probably need a loan. Let's test this plan with Meredith. We need to be clear that we are just testing the idea. We are not making a commitment, but we are asking for her help."

Aqua, Celsius, Nitro and Frostbite all slap fins.

"Congratulations," Aristotle says. "You surprised me. I thought finding a potentially viable solution would take longer."

Aristotle points to the Learn-Ideas-test-Decide chart. "These last two weeks have been a rollercoaster ride. Tomorrow morning I'd like to conduct a Learning-to-Succeed exercise to make sure we build upon what we've accomplished, and not fall back. Let's call Meredith."

Chapter 30

Team Building

"Good morning," Aristotle says as he enters the conference room. "Our first Learning-to-Succeed exercise focused on Atlantis and Dr. Bond. Today's Learning-to-Succeed exercise will focus on us. Yesterday, we identified a potential, viable solution. It's essential that we learn from our experiences. We'll start with top-of-mind thoughts. Who wants to start the discussion?"

"Plussing really works," Aqua says. "The plan to cut ice blocks off the iceberg and convey them into tankers began with Nitro's idea to wrap plastic around icebergs and let the warm water up north melt the iceberg. Celsius Plussed his idea, I Plussed Celsius' idea, and Frostbite Plussed my idea."

"That's exactly how a high-performance team works," Aristotle says. "Instead of trying to defeat ideas, win arguments, and defend ourselves against each other, high-performance teams explore lots of ideas and build on each

IMAGINE SOLVING THE MOST COMPLEX PROBLEMS

other's ideas until breakthroughs are found."

"The main thing I learned is that trust is necessary to collaborate effectively," Frostbite adds.

"Yes," Aristotle says. "Without trust, teams fall into defensive and unproductive behavior and often make poor decisions. A year or two down the road, when they realize the decision didn't work, they must start over again. The road can lead to failure even though team members are trying to do what they think is right."[17]

"Are you saying we accomplished more in two weeks than most organizations accomplish in years?" Aqua asks.

"Yes. It took Atlantis three years to find out Dr. Bond's strategy wasn't going to work. Let's talk about trust and commitment to meeting the goals of finding a safe and reliable way to extract water from icebergs that meets Hydro for Humanity's requirements."

"I tried to quit twice because I didn't trust my colleagues," Aqua says. "I was certainly not committed. I'm glad Aristotle talked me into staying."

"I was committed to building a lake on an iceberg," Celsius says. "But I was not committed to trying anything new."

"Without trust, a team has little commitment to meet ambitious goals," Aristotle says.[17]

"I like the obituaries," Frostbite says. "It gave us all a chance to raise issues."

Aristotle adds, "The obituary exercise is especially useful in drawing out issues from individuals who are quiet, like Frostbite."

"I like one-page documents better than wall charts," Aqua says. "I can take them with me and read them wherever I am. I can make notes on them."

"I like one-page documents better than wall charts too," Frostbite adds. "We can e-mail them to each other. We can mark them up electronically and send them back and forth. We can save all this paper."

Aqua looks at Aristotle. "Why did you wait so long to teach us about one-page documents?"

"Celsius, Nitro," Aristotle says. "If Frostbite sent you a one-page document as an e-mail attachment two weeks ago, would you have opened it, read it, and sent him feedback? If you had questions, would you have called him?"

After an awkward silence Nitro says, "No."

"I would now," Celsius says.

"That's because you trust one another now. Trust precedes collaboration. I started with wall charts for two reasons. First, collaboration is most effective when colleagues stand shoulder to shoulder or sit side by side. Second, I wanted you all in the room together. I wanted to observe how you interact. One-page documents are effective when team members trust each other."

"I found that drafting a one-page document helped me understand my barge idea better," Frostbite says.

Aristotle adds: "I use one-page documents to help organize my thoughts on complex topics. One-page documents can promote understanding and help keep conversations and meetings on topic."

"It helped that we met with the customer and went to the iceberg," Nitro says.

"Good point," Aristotle says. "A fundamental Lean principle is *genchi genbutsu*. It means go and see for yourself, and don't rely upon second-hand information."

Aristotle points to the Learn-Ideas-Test-Decide chart.

IMAGINE SOLVING THE MOST COMPLEX PROBLEMS

"How many trips did you make through the Learn-Ideas-Test-Decide cycle?"

"The first idea was a lakebed of ice made from heavy water and sawdust," Celsius says.

"Second was breaking the iceberg into small pieces, loading the pieces into tankers, and melting the ice en route," Nitro says.

"Third was cutting ice blocks off the iceberg, conveying the ice blocks into tankers, and melting the ice en route, with saws and conveyers secured to barges in between the iceberg and the tankers," Aqua says. "We made three trips."

"Were other alternatives considered during the three trips through the learning cycle?" Aristotle asks.

"We had two alternatives for the third idea," Frostbite says. "We evaluated securing the saws and conveyers to the iceberg in addition to securing the saws and conveyers to barges docked between the iceberg and the tankers."

"We had two different companies providing grabbers for the second idea," Aqua says.

"Celsius had five alternatives for building a lake on an iceberg," Nitro says. "The first alternative was no lakebed. There were four alternatives with lakebeds. We evaluated lakebeds of ice made from salt water, fresh water, heavy water, and heavy water and sawdust."

"As I recall," Aristotle says, "you also evaluated different lakebed thicknesses. Now that you've made three trips through the cycle, what did you learn?"

"Solutions found during the third trip through the cycle were much better than solutions found during the first and second trip through the cycle," Aqua says.

"That's how learning cycles work. The first ideas are

usually mediocre, but they have to be evaluated and learned from to find better ideas."

Aristotle draws.

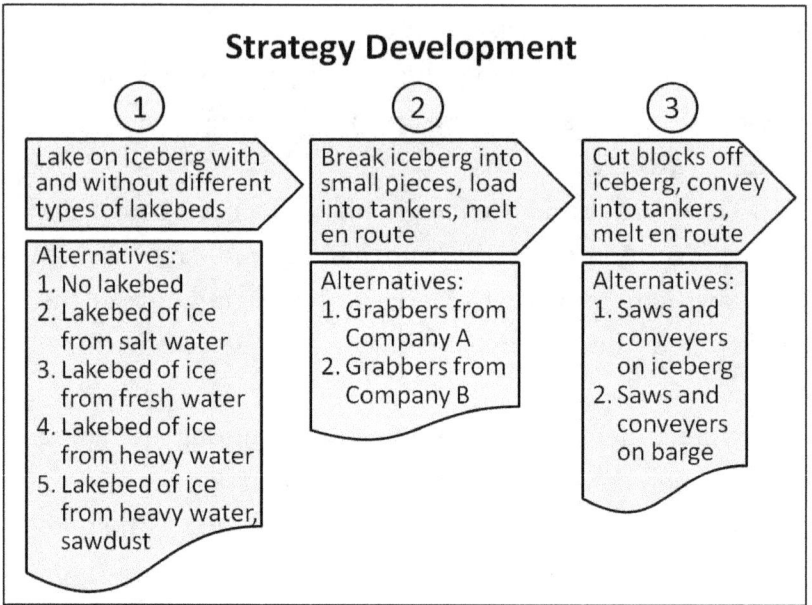

Figure 30-1

"I want you all to remember that you made three trips through the cycle in only two weeks."

Aqua walks over to the chart. "We accomplished more than I thought."

What else did you learn?" Aristotle asks.

"We could have made faster progress if we had trusted each other from the beginning," Frostbite says.

"You're right. After you trusted one another, much faster progress was made."

"How fast should we be able to move through the cycle?" Frostbite asks.

"It depends upon the complexity of the problem and how much testing has to be done. High-performance teams usually make significant progress every day."

Aristotle walks to the front of the room. "I'd like to take a thirty-minute break. When we return, we will discuss what we each learned and what we can do to improve."

Aqua walks outside. It's snowing and the wind is blowing. *Imagine trying to build a layer of ice from heavy water and sawdust in a blizzard.* She watches the snow pile up from behind a large rock that shields her from the wind.

As the wind increases, Aqua decides to reenter the building. Her phone rings. She answers.

"This is Meredith Macbeth from Hydro for Humanity. I tried to reach Aristotle, but he was unavailable."

"What can I do for you?" Aqua stutters.

"I called to tell Aristotle that the media is running stories about our project to cut ice blocks off icebergs and convey the ice blocks into tankers. He can expect calls."

"How did the press find out?"

"There are no secrets in today's world, particularly when the project is about saving millions of humans."

"I will tell him."

"Thanks," Meredith says. "Call if you need anything."

Aqua hurries back to the conference room. She is the last to arrive.

Aqua runs up to Aristotle and relays Meredith's message.

"Thank you. I spoke with the Prime Minister. She told me the same thing."

Aristotle addresses the four penguins. "The media is running stories about our project to cut ice blocks off icebergs and convey the ice blocks into tankers. Please refer any inquiries from the media to me. For the safety of journalists and sightseers, the Prime Minister will have the

Coast Guard secure the area around the iceberg."

Aristotle turns to Aqua. "I'll call Meredith and thank her. When someone raises an issue early enough that it can be resolved before it causes a big problem or failure, it's a gift. Okay. Who would like to start the discussion?"

Nitro nods. "This morning, Aqua reminded me that the Plussing started with my crazy idea to wrap icebergs in plastic and let the warm water up north melt the ice. I've spent my whole career keeping my head down and doing what I'm told. I learned I can come up with ideas myself that help."

"You certainly can come up with ideas that help," Aristotle says. "Please continue to do so."

"I will."

Frostbite takes a deep breath. "I sketched the causal diagram that showed that we can't stop icebergs from breaking a week-and-a-half before I showed it to anyone. I learned that if I don't speak up when I see issues or have ideas, then I'm part of the problem."

"Very good. What can you do to be more proactive?"

"I can write one-page documents that describe my issues and ideas and sit down with colleagues and discuss them."

"Very good," Aristotle says. "Aqua, Celsius?"

"I really wanted to implement the plan to break the iceberg into little pieces and load the pieces into tankers," Aqua says. "I was willing to trade off safety for schedule."

"Why were you willing to trade off safety for schedule?"

"I really wanted to meet Hydro for Humanity's requirements. I really wanted to save the humans."

"What did you learn?"

"I learned that my desire to meet a customer's requirements can override sound judgment. I would have felt awful if a piece of ice had sunk a ship."

"What can you do in the future to prevent yourself from trading off important requirements?"

Aqua thinks for a moment. "I can ask my colleagues what issues they see. I can do obituary exercises. I can ask colleagues to remind me if they observe me trading off important requirements again."

"Good. Celsius?"

"Our first trip through the Learn-Ideas-Test-Decide cycle was frustrating. I believed Dr. Bond's plan to build a layer of ice made from heavy water and sawdust had a good chance of meeting the challenge of finding a safe and reliable way to extract water from icebergs. Your behavior led me to believe that you didn't consider Dr. Bond's plan seriously."

Aristotle points to the gap diagram. "Then you learned that Hydro for Humanity wanted something that Dr. Bond's plan couldn't deliver. How did you react?"

"I still wanted to implement Dr. Bond's plan."

"Why did you want to implement Dr. Bond's plan even though you knew it wouldn't meet Hydro for Humanity's requirements?"

"I don't like it when goals change abruptly because it's impossible to maintain a plan of record. I become uncomfortable when there is not a plan of record."

"Is it realistic to expect that goals won't change?"

"I expect goals to change over time. But leaders should not change goals too drastically or too often because of the disruption it causes the organization."

"Do you think we should have pursued Hydro for

Humanity's requirements?"

"I don't know. It felt like Hydro for Humanity's requirements were dictated to me."

"That was my mistake," Aristotle says. "I should not have scheduled the first Decide step so soon with changing goals and just one alternative."

Aristotle pauses. "As a result, you four nearly failed as a team. By fail, I mean some of you were ready to give up."

"Why did you push us into the Decide step so soon?" Aqua asks.

"I felt pressure from the Prime Minister, the UN and Hydro for Humanity. I assumed we would make faster progress if we made decisions faster. I should have known better."

"What should you have done?"

"First, I should have told you that we needed at least three distinct alternatives. Then I should have scheduled time to discuss criteria for evaluating alternatives. We also should have discussed the importance of meeting Hydro for Humanity's requirements."

Aristotle turns to Celsius. "Would those discussions have helped?"

"Yes," Celsius says. "Those discussions would have built trust."

"Are you more comfortable with change now?"

"Yes, if we take time to discuss it."

"Can we discuss change now?" Aristotle asks.

Celsius nods.

"I'd like you to think about the changes that have happened during the last several weeks. First, the largest competitor in the fresh water industry, Atlantis, went out of business. Second, we now have a customer that wants

IMAGINE SOLVING THE MOST COMPLEX PROBLEMS

an enormous amount of fresh water right away. Third, we're about to test cutting ice blocks off an iceberg and conveying the ice blocks into tankers. No one has done that before."

Aristotle pauses to let his points sink in. "Given all this change, is it realistic to assume goals and plans won't change abruptly?"

After a moment, Celsius shakes his head. "I suppose not."

"Why not?"

"Because there is too much uncertainty?"

"Correct," Aristotle says. "We're swimming in uncertainty. How can we address uncertainty?"

Celsius looks at the Learn-Ideas-Test-Decide cycle. "We can follow the cycle. I skipped the Learn step pertaining to customer requirements."

"Were there other reasons why you wanted to move ahead with Dr. Bond's plan even though it wouldn't meet Hydro for Humanity's requirements?"

"I assumed we could not meet Hydro for Humanity's requirements. I should have tested that assumption."

"Very good. Given everything you've been through, what have you learned?"

Celsius looks down and rubs his eyes. "I learned I have tendency to make up my mind quickly and reject issues and ideas that conflict with what I assume is the right thing to do." He pauses. "My behavior was inhibiting customer satisfaction."

"What can you do in the future so that you don't make up your mind quickly and reject issues and ideas?"

"Follow the Learn-Ideas-Test-Decide cycle."

"Would it help if your colleagues reminded you to

follow the cycle?"

"Yes."

"Good." Aristotle picks up a marker. "Let's drill a little deeper into the assumptions behind your behavior. What assumptions did you make about your ability to meet the challenge of finding a safe and reliable way to extract water from icebergs that meets Hydro for Humanity's schedule requirements?"

Celsius nods. "I assumed looking for a way to meet Hydro for Humanity's schedule was a waste of time because we can't melt an iceberg in the middle of winter."

"I assumed it was not possible to safely and reliably extract water from icebergs," Aqua says. "I'm happy to be wrong about that assumption."

"I assumed it was not possible to safely and reliably extract water from icebergs also," Nitro says. "I was ready to implement any plan that would keep my job secure."

Aristotle draws.

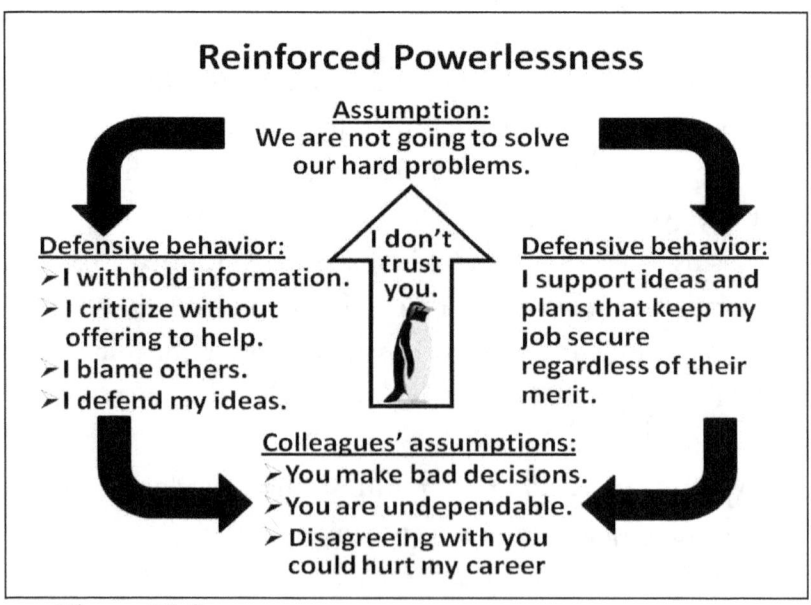

Figure 30-2

IMAGINE SOLVING THE MOST COMPLEX PROBLEMS

"See how we behave when we assume we are not going to solve our hard problems?" Aristotle says. "We support ideas and plans that keep our jobs secure regardless of their merit. We withhold information. We blame others. We defend our ideas. Our defensive behavior causes us to assume the worst about each other, which destroys trust and reinforces our assumption that we are not going to solve our hard problems. Trust is the cornerstone of a high-performance team."

"I'm starting to think we can solve any problem," Aqua says.

"Me, too," Celsius adds.

"Maybe I'm naïve," Frostbite says, "but I'm fine with not having an approved plan. To me, it makes sense to learn first, and explore and test lots of ideas before making important decisions. I assumed all along we would find a safe and reliable solution that meets Hydro for Humanity's requirements. Now that trust is stronger, we should be able to complete the Learn-Ideas-Test-Decide cycle faster."

Aristotle looks at Aqua, Celsius and Nitro. "Why do you think Frostbite assumed we could solve hard problems while the three of you assumed we couldn't?"

"Because Frostbite just started working," Aqua says. "He hasn't learned to be powerless yet."

"Let's hope he never does," Aristotle adds.

Aristotle passes out thin, three-ring binders to each of the four penguins. "I have one more tool to show you. The notebooks I just passed out are called knowledge notebooks. Knowledge notebooks are guides for solving new problems. The information in the knowledge notebooks represents what you four have learned thus far about solving iceberg problems collaboratively. Please take a moment to browse the pages."

Celsius asks, "What are knowledge notebooks for?"

"Knowledge notebooks are part of the Learn step and are used when you encounter problems, particularly complex problems."

Frostbite nods. "I like the reference material explaining the Learn-Ideas-Test-Decide chart and how to draft one-page documents and wall charts."

Aqua flips pages until she reaches the last page. "I see the causal diagram and the assumption-defensive behavior cycles. Why didn't you include the Five-Why diagrams, cause-and-effect timelines, alternative solutions, customer requirements, proposals, and obituaries?"

"Those are problem-specific or project-specific. A separate notebook will contain that information. Soon, we will have hundreds of problem-specific or project-specific documents. It's not practical to search through that much information when you face new problems. And it's not likely that you will face the exact same problems again."

"What specific types of information are included in a knowledge notebook?" Frostbite asks.

"Knowledge notebooks include reference material, rules of thumb, best practices, and relationships. Frostbite's causal diagram is included because it provides information that can be useful if someone wants to know which factors contribute to the strength and stress of icebergs. The assumption-defensive behavior cycles are included because you will most likely encounter defensive behavior again."

"I like the list of techniques for breaking the cycles of defensive behavior," Aqua says. "Why did you remove the names from the assumption-behavior cycles?"

"I removed the names because the cycles of defensive

behavior can happen to anyone. Knowing who the cycles of defensive behavior happened to in the past is not beneficial."

"How are changes or additions made to knowledge pages?" Frostbite asks.

"Since knowledge notebooks are new to you four, I will be the keeper of the knowledge. In the future, you may take turns being the keeper of the knowledge. The information in the knowledge notebook can be found in a public folder. The URL is listed in the back of the notebook. Any other questions?"

"Who prepares and maintains the project notebook?" Aqua asks.

"Would any of you like to?"

"I'd like to," Aqua says.

"Good. Let's sit down next week to get started. Anything else?"

The four penguins are silent.

"I'll see you Monday morning at eight o'clock. Have a good weekend."

Chapter 31

Dr. Hydrogen Bond Lurking Inside Us

Aristotle enters the conference room. Accompanying him are four penguins, each carrying a knowledge notebook. Aqua is briefing Celsius, Frostbite and Nitro.

New documents, prepared by Aqua, hang on the walls. Aristotle and the four penguins walk over to the wall and peruse the documents.

Aqua continues: "I talked to Meredith three times over the weekend. I haven't told her yet, but I think we can exceed her requirements if we start now. Meredith has a fleet of the largest tankers in the world. Each tanker can carry 200 thousand tons of water. We need to fill five tankers in September and forty in October."

Aqua points to a spot on the map. "The loading zone is here, 400 miles north of the Ross Ice Shelf. The whales should be able to push the iceberg there in less than three weeks. The barges with saws and conveyers will arrive at the same time, or sooner."

"Can we review blueprints of the tankers before they arrive?" Frostbite asks. "Better yet, can we go see the tankers so we know exactly what we have to work with?"

"The tankers are all the same," Aqua says, ignoring Frostbite's question. "Besides, we can build anything we need."

Aqua takes a breath. "Meredith and I decided to cut the iceberg into rectangular blocks two-feet long by two-feet wide by one-foot tall. That's a 230-pound piece of ice."

"That's nearly two million pieces of ice per tanker," Frostbite says. "Are you sure that's the best size?"

"Meredith thinks 230 pounds will be easy to handle. Here is a schedule I prepared that shows the major tasks that need to be done."

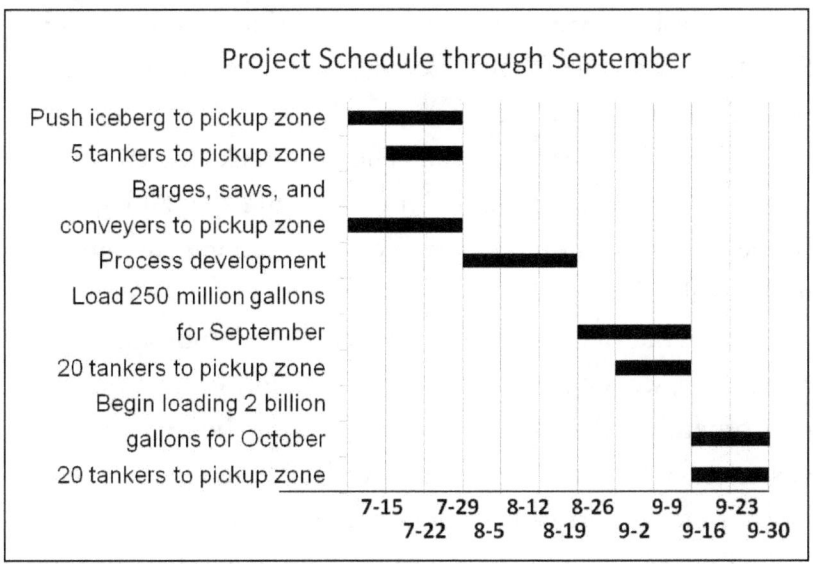

Figure 31-1

"Okay," Aristotle says. "Let's start our meeting. Aqua, it appears you worked all weekend."

"Pretty much," she says.

Aqua looks up. She recognizes two of the penguins from her interview.

"Most of you know each other," Aristotle says. "Aqua, Celsius, Frostbite, and Nitro, this is Jacuzzi, Geyser, Fjord and Lagoon. They've been working in the glacier business."

The penguins exchange pleasantries.

Aristotle continues, "I asked Jacuzzi, Geyser, Fjord and Lagoon to help figure out how to cut blocks off of icebergs and convey them into tankers."

"Is that necessary?" Aqua asks. "We've decided on the size of the ice blocks. We have a schedule showing that we will achieve the shipments required for September and October. I think we have the project under control."

"Are you sure the ice block size you selected will work? Aristotle asks. "Are you sure your schedule is achievable? Shouldn't we follow the Learn-Ideas-Test-Decide cycle before making important decisions?"

"We can't afford to wait. The ice-block-size decision drives everything: the size of the saws, the size and speed of the conveyers, and the design of the handling equipment in the tanker."

"Yes, the ice-block-size decision is important. But remember, we are still in the test phase, and we're trying to do something that has never been done before, with a customer we've never worked with. Would you rather invest time and effort now to figure out what will work, or make the key decisions now and find out later whether they work when the whole world is watching?"

"But things are going amazingly …Oh no!" Aqua shrieks.

Aqua gasps.

"Are you all right?" Aristotle says.

IMAGINE SOLVING THE MOST COMPLEX PROBLEMS

"I'm ...," Aqua says, wheezing. "I'm turning into Dr. Hydrogen Bond. I've got Mad Emperor's Disease!"

"You're fine," Aristotle says reassuringly. "You're excited because you're talking to the Chairman of the Board of an important customer about an important project. The fact that you realize success was beginning to go to your head means you don't have Mad Emperor's Disease."

Aqua takes a deep breath, sits down, and sighs.

Aristotle addresses the group. "We must never stop testing our assumptions because there's a little bit of Dr. Hydrogen Bond lurking inside all of us."

Part V Summary

As soon as defensive behavior was turned into collaborative behavior, Aqua, Celsius, Frostbite and Nitro began raising issues, sharing ideas, asking for help, and exchanging know-how. Disagreements resulted in better ideas, instead of resentment and paralysis.

Frostbite demonstrated his new collaborative behavior by meeting privately with Celsius to explain why, with the help of a causal diagram, the assumption that they could prevent icebergs from breaking is false.

Frostbite also came up with a solution to that problem: a barge docked between the iceberg and the tanker so that icebergs can break without risking injury and supply interruptions.

The problem was solved. Aqua's fear of running around screaming "Iceberg Down" was alleviated.

Aristotle conducted a Learning-to-Succeed exercise that revealed:

IMAGINE SOLVING THE MOST COMPLEX PROBLEMS

1. Once Aqua, Celsius, Frostbite and Nitro started trusting each other, the team made rapid progress.
2. Three Learn-Ideas-Test-Decide cycle were completed in two weeks.
3. The quality of the solutions improved significantly from the first Learn-Ideas-Test-Decide cycle to the third.
4. It was helpful to visit the customer and perform experiments on an iceberg.

The most significant revelations were: trust precedes collaboration, and trust precedes commitment to ambitious goals.

Aristotle explained that he started with wall charts because collaboration is most effective when colleagues stand shoulder to shoulder or sit side by side. He also wanted to observe how the four penguins interacted.

With trust established, Aristotle encouraged the penguins to use one-page documents to:

1. Promote understanding.
2. Keep conversations and meetings on topic.
3. Enable effective communication when meeting face to face isn't possible.

After a break, the penguins shared what they had learned about themselves:

1. After spending his whole career keeping his head down and doing what he's told, Nitro learned he can come up with ideas that help. He pledged to continue to raise issues and offer ideas.
2. After waiting a week-and-a-half to show his causal diagram to anyone, Frostbite learned that if he

doesn't speak up when he sees issues or has ideas, then he's part of the problem. He agreed to write one-page documents that describe his issues and ideas and discuss them with colleagues.
3. Aqua learned that her desire to meet customers' requirements can override sound judgment. To prevent trading off important requirements, Aqua will ask her colleagues to raise issues; she will do obituary exercises; and her colleagues will remind her if they observe her trading off important requirements again.
4. By pushing to implement Dr. Bond's plan to build a layer of ice made from heavy water and sawdust even though it didn't meet Hydro for Humanity's requirements, Celsius learned that he has a tendency to jump to conclusions and reject issues that conflict with what he decided is the right thing to do. To prevent himself from jumping to conclusions, Celsius agreed to follow the Lean-Ideas-Test-Decide cycle. His colleagues will remind him if they observe him jumping to conclusions again.

Initially, Celsius blamed his frustration on Aristotle for changing goals abruptly. Celsius said leaders should not change goals too drastically or too often because of the disruption it causes the organization. Celsius also said he wanted to implement Dr. Bond's plan because he believed it had a good chance of meeting the challenge of finding a safe and reliable way to extract water from icebergs.

Aristotle took responsibility for the problem. He said that he should not have scheduled the first Decide step so soon with changing goals and just one alternative. Aristotle admitted that he felt pressure from the Prime Minister, the UN and Hydro for Humanity.

Aristotle stated that he should have explained that at least three alternatives were needed, and he should have spent time discussing criteria for evaluating alternatives and the importance of meeting Hydro for Humanity's requirements.

Aristotle reminded Celsius of the changes that had occurred during the last several weeks:

1. The largest competitor in the fresh water industry, Atlantis, went out of business.
2. Glacier Fresh Water now has a customer that wants an enormous amount of fresh water right away.
3. The four penguins are about to test a brand new method for extracting water from icebergs.

Celsius then acknowledged that it's not realistic to expect that goals and plans won't change abruptly because there is too much uncertainty.

Celsius realized that he skipped the Learn step pertaining to customer requirements and made the assumption that Hydro for Humanity's requirements could not be met.

By taking responsibility for the problem, Aristotle was able to help Celsius see how his behavior was inhibiting customer satisfaction and how to improve.

Aristotle asked what assumptions drove their behavior. Aqua, Celsius and Nitro said that they assumed a safe and reliable method of extracting water from icebergs that would meet Hydro for Humanity's requirements would not be found. Aristotle showed how that assumption drove defensive behavior that led colleagues to assume the worst about each other, which destroyed trust and reinforced the assumption that hard problems would not be solved.

Frostbite, the least experienced of the four, assumed all along that a safe and reliable method of extracting water from icebergs that would meet Hydro for Humanity's requirements would be found.

Success started to go to Aqua's head because she was talking to Meredith Macbeth, Chairman of the Board of Hydro for Humanity, about providing fresh water to save millions of humans.

Aristotle reminded the group that they must never stop testing their assumptions because there is a little bit of Dr. Hydrogen Bond lurking inside all of us.

Epilogue: High-Performance Organization
Chapter 32: Decision Day
August 22

"Welcome," Aristotle says, standing in the front of the small make-shift conference room on one of the two barges. Each barge is sandwiched between the five-mile-long iceberg and a 200-thousand-gallon tanker. Eight members of the two teams stand facing him.

Aristotle points to the chart showing when important decision will be made.

"Today we decide what commitment we will make to Hydro for Humanity for the month of September. Next week, we will order equipment and finalize staffing plans for October's production. Remember, Hydro for Humanity treats a commitment as a guarantee. We don't want to commit to anything without strong evidence that we can meet our commitment."

Aristotle looks around the room. "We have two teams. Aqua, Celsius, Nitro and Frostbite make up one team. Jacuzzi, Geyser, Fjord and Lagoon make up the other. Each team has its own barge and tanker. Who would like to go first?"

Project Milestone Schedule

Decision	Aug.	Sept.	Oct.	Nov.	Dec.
Hydro for Humanity Demand (gallons)	0	250 million	2.0 billion	4.0 billion	6.0 billion
Monthly Fresh Water Commitment	8-22 for Sept.	9-22 for Oct.	10-22 for Nov.	11-22 for Dec.	12-22 for Jan.
Finalize staffing & hiring plans for monthly capacity	8-27 for Sept.	9-27 for Oct.	10-27 for Nov.	11-27 for Dec.	12-27 for Jan.
Order barges, saws, conveyer for month	8-28 for Sept.	9-28 for Oct.	10-28 for Nov.	11-28 for Dec.	12-28 for Jan.

Figure 32-1

"We will," Celsius says. "I want to remind everyone that we are responsible for loading ice into the tankers. Hydro for Humanity is responsible for melting the ice."

"That is correct," Aristotle says. "But if the ice doesn't melt in time, it will reflect badly upon us. Has anyone reviewed Hydro for Humanity's plan for melting the ice?"

"It's a two-pronged plan," Frostbite says. "First, Hydro for Humanity has brand new, single hull tankers, not double hull like most oil tankers. The warm ocean water up north will transmit heat through the metal hull to the ice. Second, the tanker crew plans to blow warm tropical air across the ice. Once the tankers reach the tropics, the ice will melt rapidly. I checked their calculations, and they included a large margin for error."

"Do we have enough spare parts?" Aristotle ask.

"Yes," Nitro says. "The saw blades and the saw motors are all the same size. The conveyer belts, rollers, and motors also come in standard sizes. We have a healthy inventory of every part that can break. I have a spread sheet. Would you like to see it?"

Aristotle nods. "Please send it to me."

Celsius and Aqua attach their chart to the wall. "We loaded blocks of ice equivalent to 39 million gallons of water," Celsius announces. "We're more than 15 percent of the way to September's 250-million-gallon requirement."

"We've done several trial runs," Aqua adds. "In a two-shift day, we can average 15 million gallons a day. That's 330 million gallons for September, assuming twenty-two work days, plus the 39 million we already loaded, for a total of 369 million gallons."

"We can easily exceed the September goal by ourselves," Celsius says.

"Very good," Aristotle says. All the penguins applaud.

"How many experiments did you run?" Aristotle asks.

"Ten," Celsius says.

"Actually seven," Frostbite says. "We had to repeat three because we made mistakes the first time."

"Those seven trips through Learn-Ideas-Test-Decide cycle taught us how to improve throughput by 70 percent," Celsius adds.

"What was size of your ice blocks?" Aristotle asks.

"We did a few experiments and settled on ice blocks that are two-feet long by two-feet wide and one-foot tall," Aqua answers. "We wanted a square base so we could load the ice blocks in either direction. Although we would have liked to cut larger ice blocks, we decided to keep the weight down for safety."

"What are your top problems?" Aristotle asks.

Aqua points to the next bullet. "Our biggest problem was loading the tanker because the ice blocks slid when waves were large enough to rock the tanker. We had to slow down the process of cutting and conveying ice, and loading the tanker several times because we were afraid the ice blocks would slide off the stack of ice and hurt someone."

Frostbite adds, "If it's windy for several days, our production could be significantly reduced."

Aristotle walks over to the wall chart. "When you say you can load the equivalent of 15 million gallons per day, does that assume waves are small enough that the ice blocks won't slide in the tanker?"

"Fifteen million gallons per day is our average," Frostbite says. "The variation is large because we slowed down several times during our trial runs."

"Can you calculate a production rate with a 95 percent confidence level?" Aristotle asks.

Frostbite examines a spreadsheet on his laptop.

Aristotle turns to Aqua. "You identified the issue of ice shifting in tankers during the obituary exercise."

"I know."

Frostbite raises his fin. "At a confidence level of 95 percent, we can average six million gallons per day, or 132 million for September. Adding the 39 million we already loaded, we can produce a total of 171 million."

"Is that all?" Celsius asks.

"The large variation in trial run production brings the production rate down when a 95 percent confident level is applied."

Aristotle looks at Aqua, Celsius, Frostbite and Nitro. "Excellent work. Jacuzzi, let's see your results."

Jacuzzi stands. "I want to thank Aqua, Celsius, Frostbite and Nitro for teaching us about icebergs and for taking us with them to visit the tankers, saws and conveyers. Viewing the operations for ourselves was helpful. Icebergs are new to us."

Jacuzzi and Geyser attach their chart to the wall and reveal only the first bullet.

"We loaded ice equivalent to eleven million gallons of water," Jacuzzi says.

They reveal the next bullet. "We conducted thirty-three experiments."

"Did you have to redo any?" Celsius asks.

"No," says Jacuzzi.

"At a confidence level of 95 percent, we can load 47 million gallons a day on two shifts."

"Forty-seven million gallons per day!" Aqua exclaims. "That's over a billion gallons for the month."

"What was your average?" Frostbite asks.

"We averaged 52 thousand gallons a minute," Jacuzzi says. "We did trial runs for ten or twenty minutes. That's 3.1 million gallons per hour, or 50 million per day."

"Wow," Nitro says.

"We were measuring by the hour, and you were measuring by the minute," Aqua says.

"What was size of your ice blocks?" Celsius asks.

Jacuzzi answers. "Lagoon came up with the idea of variable ice block size. All ice blocks are one-meter wide and a half-meter tall, but the length varies. We use short ice blocks loaded at a slower speed to build a frame inside the tanker. Then we use long ice blocks loaded at a faster speed to fill the tanker. Our longest ice blocks were three-meters long."

"That's over 3,000 pounds," Frostbite says."

"Once the frame is built, we can load the tanker pretty fast," Lagoon says.

"The penguin inside the tanker orders ice blocks in the length needed," Geyser adds.

"Several experiments were required to work out the bugs. The variable-length-ice-block idea doubled throughput by itself."

"What about ice blocks sliding?" Aqua asks. "A 3,000-pound ice block could kill somebody if it slides off the stack."

"We found a solution to the ice block sliding problem," Jacuzzi says. "I sent you all e-mail messages two days ago."

Aqua, Celsius, Frostbite and Nitro look at their phones and nod.

"Sorry," Aqua says. "I was so busy I didn't check my e-mail carefully."

Jacuzzi continues. "The solution was in the knowledge notebook Aristotle gave us. The causal diagram listed sawdust as a factor that increases tensile strength. We found that blowing heated sawdust on the ice blocks already stacked in the tanker, just before we place new ice blocks on top of the stacked ice blocks, solves the sliding problem. The heated sawdust melts the ice on the surface where the ice blocks contact each other. The surface quickly refreezes."

"Sawdust turns ice blocks into a concrete wall," Geyser says, "instantly."

"How will the sawdust be removed from the water after the ice melts?" Aqua asks.

"We had a conference call with Hydro for Humanity," Jacuzzi says. "Hydro for Humanity plans to conduct

IMAGINE SOLVING THE MOST COMPLEX PROBLEMS

experiments over the next few days in Christchurch. Geyser prepared a one-page document describing the sliding problem, its causes, alternative solutions, and next steps. It was attached to the e-mail I sent you all."

"I read it in Penguin City," Aristotle says. "Well done. Do Dalton and Meredith agree that blowing sawdust onto the stacked ice is the right thing to do?"

"I think so," Geyser says. "The engineers from Hydro for Humanity that were on the phone call support blowing sawdust onto the stacked ice. Neither Dalton nor Meredith were on the phone call."

"I'll follow up with Meredith and Dalton to make sure they support the practice," Aristotle says.

"Is the amount of sawdust important?" Frostbite asks.

"Yes," Fjord says. "But after a certain point, adding more sawdust doesn't increase the strength of the bond between ice blocks. The curve looks like this."[18]

Fjord draws.

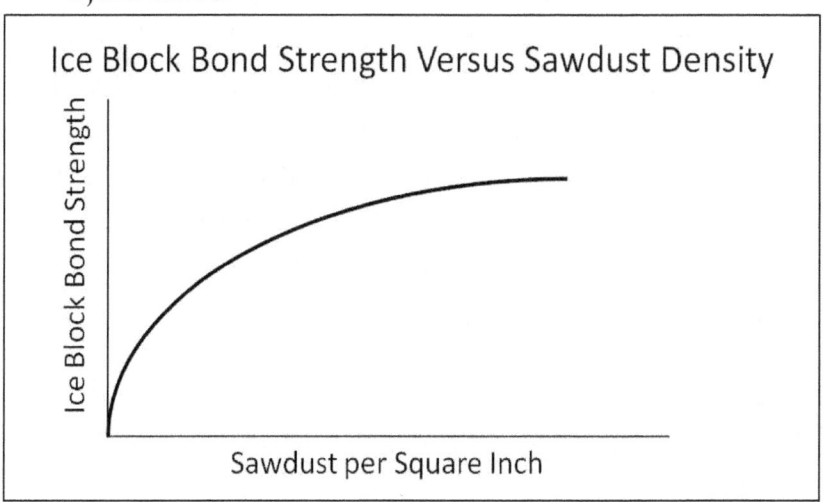

Figure 32-2

"Sawdust is cheap," Celsius says. "Does it make sense to

err on the side of too much sawdust?"

Fjord answers: "You're right. Sawdust is cheap. But heating and blowing sawdust onto the stacked ice costs money. Removing sawdust from melted water also costs money. We don't want to spend money unnecessarily."

"What's the ideal temperature of the sawdust?" Frostbite asks Fjord.

"We don't know for sure. We've done a few experiments. We expect to find that increasing the temperature beyond a certain point doesn't increase the bond strength. We plan to run more experiments next week."

"I imagine sawdust cools pretty fast," Frostbite says. "How long can you wait between the time the sawdust lands on the stack and the new ice blocks are loaded?"

"Yes, sawdust cools very quickly, particularly when it contacts ice. We're trying to minimize the time between the sawdust landing on the surface of ice blocks already stacked and placing new ice blocks on the stack. A problem with blowing sawdust is that the slightest draft causes the sawdust to miss the surface we're aiming for."

"Did you consider mixing the sawdust with warm water and spraying it on the ice blocks?" Frostbite asks.

"That's a good idea. We didn't think of that."

"What made you look for the solution in the knowledge notebook?" Aqua asks.

Jacuzzi smiles. "The Learn step of Learn-Ideas-Test-Decide process includes checking knowledge notebooks for potential solutions."

"What are your top problems?" Aristotle asks.

Jacuzzi and Geyser attach another chart to the wall.

"Here are the top ten problems in priority order,"

Jacuzzi says. "Our top priority problem is figuring out how to synchronize the speed of the barge, tanker, and saws, as the saws move back and forth along the iceberg. Our second priority problem is optimizing the sawdust process that holds ice blocks together in the tanker. Third, improving accuracy of ice-block-length ordering process. We are continually surprised when the ice blocks entering the tanker are different from what we thought was ordered. You can read the rest. You'll find a one-page document on each problem."

"Very good," Aristotle says. "I'll tell Meredith and Dalton we can provide the equivalent of 1.2 billion gallons in September. Meredith said she has enough tankers for six billion gallons per month, so 1.2 billion gallons shouldn't be a problem."

Aristotle walks over to the financial analysis wall chart. "Factoring in revenue from 1.2 billion gallons in September, net cash flow is positive in September. We can copy Jacuzzi's process and load two billion gallons in October. I'll add some cost for unforeseen expenses. Cumulative cash flow is positive in November. We don't need a loan."

Financial Analysis

($000)	Aug	Sept	Oct	Nov	Dec	Jan	Feb
Revenue	0	24	40	80	120	120	120
Cost	20	20	25	50	75	75	75
Net cash flow	(20)	4	15	30	45	45	45
Cumulative cash flow	(20)	(16)	(1)	29	74	119	164

Figure 32-3

Aristotle stares at the numbers.

"Too much profit?" Geyser asks.

Aristotle smiles. "We have an opportunity to improve customer satisfaction. I'll tell Meredith and Dalton we may be able reduce the price. That will offset Hydro for Humanity's cost of removing sawdust from the water and, hopefully, help provide more water to customers faster. We can't have too many satisfied customers."

"I can't imagine Dr. Bond or Colonel Tierney saying the words 'too much profit'," Celsius says.

Aqua looks at Aristotle. "I'm curious. What do you think about Dr. Bond's perfect synergistic strategy?"

"I agree with what you four said during the first Learning-to-Succeed exercise. The lake of fresh water was used to help the resort make money. As a result, customer satisfaction was sacrificed. Anytime an organization sacrifices customer satisfaction or even stops trying its hardest to improve customer satisfaction, it opens the door to competitors. Sooner or later profit will decrease. My approach to business is simple: relentlessly improve customer satisfaction, and make enough money to pay the bills and build more high-performance teams."

Celsius looks at the financial analysis chart. "I'm surprised by how much profit we can make selling fresh water. Dr. Bond and Colonel Tierney assumed providing water to humans would not make enough profit."

"That assumption led Dr. Bond to build the resort and delay draining the lake," Nitro adds.

"That assumption turned out to be false," Aqua says.

Geyser adds, "I believe high-performance teams can earn more profit through superior customer satisfaction than can be earned any other way."

IMAGINE SOLVING THE MOST COMPLEX PROBLEMS

"May I draw something?" Aqua asks. Aristotle nods.

Figure 32-4

Aqua explains: "I think this chart shows what you're saying. We build high-performance teams. High-performance teams solve complex problems. We achieve superior customer satisfaction and make enough money to pay the bills and build more high-performance teams."

"I like your chart," Aristotle says. "Succeeding with high-performance teams really is that simple. We built a high-performance team in the glacier business. The high-performance team achieved superior customer satisfaction. We made enough money to build more high-performance teams and expand into icebergs."

Aristotle checks his watch. "I'm going to call Meredith. Let's reconvene in thirty minutes and discuss what we learned."

Chapter 33

High-Performance Organization

Aristotle hurries into the conference room. "I just spoke with Meredith and Dalton. They are pleased with our commitment to provide 1.2 billion gallons of water in September. Meredith and Dalton were not aware of the sawdust removal step. With the help of the one-page document, I was able to talk them through it. They support our sawdust solution."

"Sorry," Geyser says. "I thought Meredith and Dalton knew about the sawdust."

Aristotle continues: "Today's Learning-to-Succeed exercise focuses on what we've learned and what we're going to do to perform better. Let's start with top-of-mind thoughts. Who wants to start the discussion?"

"I learned we focused on the wrong thing," Aqua says. "We spent most of our time loading the tanker. We should have been following the Learn-Ideas-Test-Decide cycle to solve problems and improve the process."

"I should have read our knowledge notebook,"

Frostbite says. "You guys used our knowledge to solve the ice-block-sliding problem."

"We've been using a knowledge notebook in the glacier business for a long time," Fjord says, glancing at Aristotle.

"No secrets," Aristotle says.

"When Aristotle gave us the iceberg knowledge notebooks, I asked him who prepared the knowledge. He said he did. I knew I could trust the information because Aristotle prepared it."

Aristotle adds, "If colleagues don't trust the author of the knowledge notebook, the knowledge is not likely to be used."

Aqua looks at Jacuzzi. "Can you tell us about your process?"

"First, we didn't try to load ice into a tanker. We focused on problem solving and process improvement. Before we do an experiment, we always write a detailed plan on a one-page document. We all review the plan before we start in order to avoid mistakes."

Jacuzzi points to a wall chart.

	Daily Standup Meeting					
	Mon. 8-27	Tue. 8-28	Wed. 8-29	Thur. 8-23	Friday 8-24	Next Week
Jacuzzi	☐ ☐	☐	☐ ☐	☐	☐ ☐	☐ ☐ ☐
Geyser	☐	☐ ☐		☐ ☐ ☐	☐	☐ ☐ ☐ ☐
Fjord	☐ ☐		☐ ☐	☐		☐ ☐ ☐ ☐
Lagoon		☐ ☐ ☐	☐		☐ ☐	☐ ☐ ☐

Figure 33-1

"Experiments can be logistical nightmares, so we break the tasks down and assign owners. We review every task in our daily standup meeting. We use this simple wall chart with a column for each day of the week and an owner for each row. The chart shows the tasks due over the next five days plus tasks due the following week. It's a rolling one-week schedule. Each task is written on a note in the cell corresponding to the owner and the due date."

Geyser adds: "When tasks are behind schedule, we work together to fix whatever problems are causing the delay. We all review the results of experiments and decide what to do next."

Jacuzzi points to another wall chart. "We also maintain a simple run chart that shows our throughput progress. We plot a point every time we complete a learning cycle. It helps us see our improvement and rate of improvement. As you can see, the majority of our throughput improvement came from variable size ice blocks and blowing saw dust on the ice stacked in the tanker."

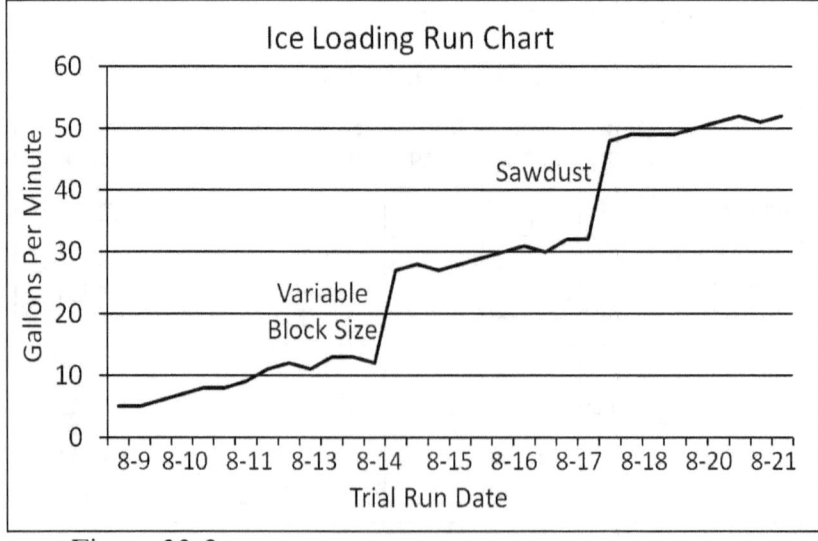

Figure 33-2

IMAGINE SOLVING THE MOST COMPLEX PROBLEMS

"What time is your morning meeting?" Aqua asks.

"Seven-fifteen," Jacuzzi says. "The standup meeting lasts about fifteen minutes. We have a problem-solving meeting right after the standup meeting."

Aqua turns to Jacuzzi and Geyser. "I met you both when I interviewed, and you were so modest. I had no idea you were such high performers."

"Are the others in the glacier business as good as you guys?" Frostbite asks.

"Jacuzzi, Geyser, Fjord and Lagoon are the highest performers," Aristotle says. "They make any team they're on more effective because their collaborative behavior is contagious."

Aristotle looks at each penguin. "Let's take a thirty-minute break. When we return, we will discuss what you each learned."

Aqua walks outside. It's an unusually warm winter day. The sun is bright in the north sky. She climbs the ladder from the barge to the iceberg and walks over to the saws. At twelve feet in diameter, the saws are imposing. The first saw makes a vertical cut parallel to the side of the iceberg that determines the width of the ice block. The second saw makes a horizontal cut that determines the height of the ice block. The third saw makes a vertical cut that determines the length of the ice block. A large wedge kicks the ice blocks onto the conveyer. Aqua checks her watch and hurries back to the conference room.

"Who would like to start the discussion?"

"I learned to appreciate the power of visibility tools and processes," Frostbite says. "You guys used our knowledge to solve an iceberg problem. Your process for managing experiments is very efficient. I'm hoping we can run experiments while we're in full production."

"I hope we can too," Aristotle says. "Processes either improve or they slide back. We want to continually improve the process. Who's next?"

Nitro nods. "I was reluctant to experiment with different ice block sizes because I was more concerned with loading the tanker. I learned I have to trust the Learn-Ideas-Test-Decide cycle. You guys trusted the cycle and significantly improved the ice block cutting, conveying, and loading process."

"Very good," Aristotle says. "I'm going to combine Frostbite's insights with Nitro's insights. He draws.

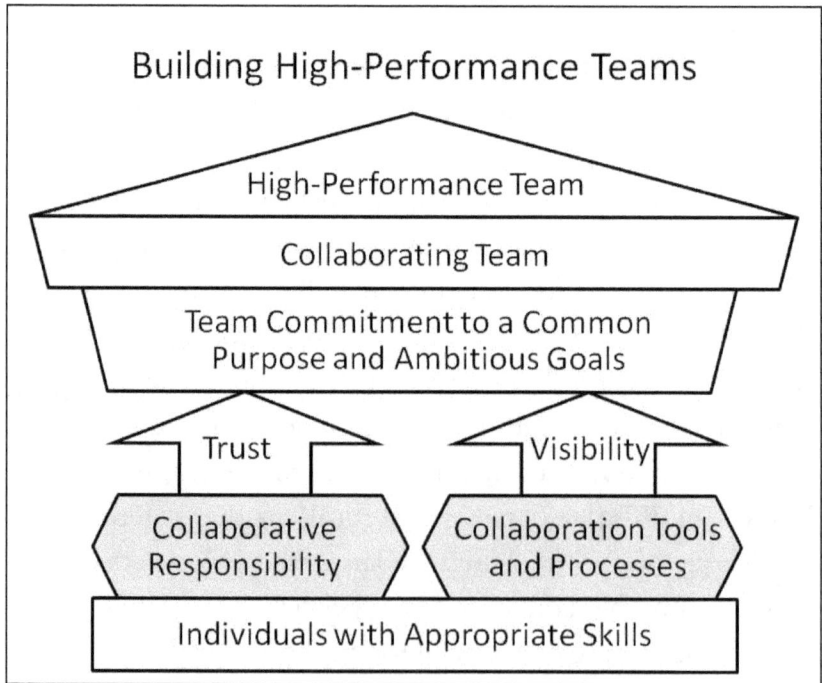

Figure 33-3

"Aqua, Celsius, Nitro and Frostbite started as individuals with the appropriate skills. But initially, they didn't perform well as a team because of their experience at

IMAGINE SOLVING THE MOST COMPLEX PROBLEMS

Atlantis."

"I had the same problem when I started here," Fjord says.

"Aqua, Celsius, Nitro and Frostbite had to learn collaborative responsibility and collaboration tools and processes. Collaborative responsibility builds trust. Collaboration tools and processes are used to make problems and opportunities visible before, as well as after, important decisions are made. Trust and visibility are required for teams to commit to a common purpose and ambitious goals."

Aristotle turns to Aqua, Celsius, Nitro and Frostbite. "You four have become what I call a collaborating team. Collaborating teams have enough trust and visibility to raise issues, admit mistakes, ask for help, and share ideas and know-how. Collaborating teams improve performance primarily by integrating the best ideas from the team members. Would you agree?"

"I agree," Frostbite says. "We've mainly taken advantage of what we already knew or found out individually."

Aristotle continues: "High-performance teams go further. In addition to integrating team members' best ideas, high-performance teams quickly and continually move through the Learn-Ideas-Test-Decide cycle, uncovering better solutions each time, until breakthroughs are found that create customer-valued innovation and new know-how. As a result, high-performance teams far exceed their goals."

"For me," Lagoon says, "the best part of working with this team is that work is fun. I can raise any issue or suggest any idea and be with colleagues who are totally comfortable discussing it."

"Before joining us," Aristotle says, "Lagoon worked at a

company a lot like Atlantis."

Lagoon adds: "Now I realize how draining it was to always have my defenses up. I worried about raising issues that my boss might find threatening. I wondered if what colleagues said was really what they believed."

"For me," Fjord says, "the best part of working with this team is that ideas are constantly in the air."

Aristotle looks at Aqua, Celsius, Nitro and Frostbite. "You four have the skills required to become a high-performance team. Okay. Who would like to go next?"

Celsius nods. "I used to think the ideal leader listens to input and then makes decisions. In business school, this type of leader was called a participative leader. Dr. Bond, however, was an autocratic leader. He made decisions, but he didn't listen."

Celsius turns to Aristotle. "I expected you to be a participative leader. You listened, but you didn't make decisions. Instead of making decisions, you continually asked us to repeat the Learn-Ideas-Test-Decide cycle. I found your indecision frustrating."

Celsius turns to Jacuzzi. "After seeing what your team accomplished, I realize high-performance teams can far outperform autocratic and participative leaders."

"What surprised you about Jacuzzi's team?"

"I was surprised by the speed of improvement and the self-management of Jacuzzi's team."

"What did you learn?"

"I learned that when faced with complex problems, high-performance teams are superior because they rapidly complete learning cycles that solve problems, test assumptions, and develop better solutions."

"A big difference between collaborating teams and high-

IMAGINE SOLVING THE MOST COMPLEX PROBLEMS

performance teams is that high-performance teams have enough trust and visibility to continually and quickly complete Learn-Ideas-Test-Decide cycles. Collaborating teams usually require encouragement to repeat the cycle. Without encouragement, collaborating teams are more likely to integrate team members best ideas and move into implementation, when another quick trip or two through the cycle would produce a much better solution. Did you learn about teams in business school?"

"I was taught that teams should only be used as a last resort because teams are typically slow to make progress, difficult to control, and often dysfunctional. I studied several examples of teams failing. In business school, the focus was on decision-making processes, not solving complex problems."

"When problems are straight-forward, decision-making processes can help," Aristotle says. "It's difficult to imagine how superior high-performance teams are until you are part of one or observe one."

"Isn't the advantage of autocratic leadership the ability to make decisions fast?" Nitro asks.

"Yes," Aristotle says. "Autocratic leadership is appropriate when decision-making speed is essential. There are also many situations when participative leaders make decisions that are good enough."[19]

Aqua shakes her head. "When we started working for Aristotle, we were a dysfunctional team. The wall charts made the problems visible and understandable, but we didn't have enough trust to collaborate. Consequently, we were not committed to the goals, and we made little progress."

"Dysfunctional teams are the worst," Jacuzzi says,

"because success relies upon colleagues who don't trust each other."

Aristotle adds: "Management teams can be dysfunctional if managers are held individually accountable for results and individual results are more important than team results. Individual accountability can promote defensive behavior that can defeat the changes managers know they need to make."

"How do you define a team?" Nitro asks.

"A team is defined as two or more individuals committed to a common purpose or mission and who rely upon each other for success," Aristotle says. "Because the roles on a team are interdependent, team members share responsibility for success."

"When are high-performance teams needed?" Aqua asks.

Aristotle answers: "High-performance teams are needed when problems contain a high degree of complexity, interdependence or uncertainty. In business, these types of problems are often found in strategy development, product and process development, customer service, market development, and operations. Many schools and universities have problems that require high-performance teams. So do government agencies, non-governmental organizations, and communities."

"Sounds as if problems with a high degree of complexity, interdependence or uncertainty are everywhere," Aqua says.

Geyser adds, "Figuring out how to safely and reliably extract water from icebergs in the middle of the winter is a good example of a complex problem."

Celsius turns to Aristotle. "What about accountability?

IMAGINE SOLVING THE MOST COMPLEX PROBLEMS

Don't leaders have to hold teams accountable?"

"That's true for autocratic leaders, participative leaders, and dysfunctional teams. Collaborating and high-performance team members hold each other accountable. Because our employees want to be part of high-performance teams, the team members are self-motivated. Team members want to improve their performance and meet the challenge. The self-motivation makes my job easier."

Aristotle nods to Celsius. "Good insight. Good discussion. Aqua?"

"When Aristotle first told me about collaborative responsibility, I was skeptical. I never dreamed I could influence the behavior of my colleagues. But now I realize that if I take responsibility for everyone's success and help resolve my colleagues' issues and worries, I can make a big difference. Collaborative behavior empowers me to solve complex problems and satisfy customers."

"Point well taken," Aristotle says. "Collaborative behavior can be very powerful," Aristotle says. "Jacuzzi, Geyser, Fjord, Lagoon, what have you learned?"

"I learned I should have invited Aqua to our conference call with Hydro for Humanity," Geyser says. "Aqua has a relationship with Meredith. She would have made sure Meredith and Dalton knew about the sawdust solution to ice blocks slipping."

"Good," Aristotle says. "Who's next?"

Fjord looks at Aqua, Celsius, Nitro and Frostbite. "I should have called you guys when we were brainstorming solutions to the ice-blocks-sliding-in-the-tanker problem. We would have found a better solution."

"That's correct," Aristotle says. "When brainstorming,

you can't have too many brains."

Lagoon nods. "I should have enlisted Aqua, Celsius, Nitro and Frostbite's help on the ice-block-size experiments. Now that we're using sawdust to prevent ice blocks from slipping, we may be able to cut taller ice blocks without worrying about them sliding off the stack."

"Jacuzzi?" Aristotle says.

Jacuzzi takes a deep breath. "Before the break I was proud that we developed a process that can produce a billion gallons of fresh water a month. During the break, Aqua's diagram showing high-performance teams delivering superior customer satisfaction hit me. Our company succeeds by building high-performance teams. Aside from Aristotle, I'm the senior penguin here. I should have taken collaborative responsibility for all eight of us by proposing that we combine teams and become one team of eight. By not collaborating, we missed our greatest opportunity to provide customer satisfaction."

"Jacuzzi's right," Geyser announces. "If we had collaborated, our September commitment would be at least two billion gallons."

Fjord quickly turns to Jacuzzi and Geyser. "We weren't asked to collaborate. We were asked to develop a safe and reliable process that meets the customer's requirements. We did what we were asked."

"Fjord," Lagoon says. "You're becoming defensive."

Fjord straightens. "You're right. Sorry."

"Fjord's correct," Aristotle says. "I asked you to develop a safe and reliable process that meets the customer's requirements. You achieved that goal. I did not ask you to collaborate. Remember, the purpose of Learning-to-Succeed exercises is to improve. You should all be proud of what you've accomplished. You should also be proud that you're learning how to perform even better."

Aristotle pauses. "I want to thank Fjord and Lagoon for demonstrating how high-performance team members hold each other accountable."

Aristotle turns to the whole group. "Did any of you discuss collaborating between teams?"

"I thought about it," Jacuzzi says. "But we were busy, and we were making good progress."

"I'm curious," Aristotle says to Jacuzzi. "When you thought about collaborating with Aqua, Celsius, Nitro and Frostbite, did you assume collaborating would help or hurt your team's performance?"

"I assumed we were under pressure to achieve our goals and that collaborating would slow us down. I should have tested that assumption. I should have given collaboration a chance."

"I didn't even read Jacuzzi's e-mail," Aqua says. "I didn't want anything to interfere with our progress. I never dreamed Jacuzzi, Geyser, Fjord and Lagoon were a high-performance team."

Frostbite holds up a sheet of paper. "A few weeks ago I started a one-page proposal to collaborate. I figured Jacuzzi's team could help us because they've been practicing high performance longer than we have."

"Did you show it to anyone?" Aristotle asks.

"He showed it to me," Aqua says. "We had just performed a few good trial runs. I discouraged Frostbite from pursuing collaboration with Jacuzzi's team because I assumed we could meet Hydro for Humanity's requirements by ourselves. That assumption turned out to be false."

"Did any of you assume that you were competing with

the other team," Aristotle asks.

"I did," Celsius says. "I wanted to prove we could meet the September commitment by ourselves."

"Me too," Aqua says. "I thought it was our responsibility to meet Hydro for Humanity's requirements."

"I did too," Fjord says. "I'm a competitive guy."

Jacuzzi and Geyser nod.

"It's easy for teams to compete against each other," Lagoon says.

"Yes, it is," Aristotle says. "Team members assumed they were under pressure to achieve their goals and that collaborating would have slowed down their teams. Instead of collaborating, the two teams competed. Customer satisfaction was sub-optimized. Sub-optimized customer satisfaction can reinforce the assumptions that teams are under pressure to meet goals and that collaboration will slow them down. Let me show you a reinforcing cycle of competition."

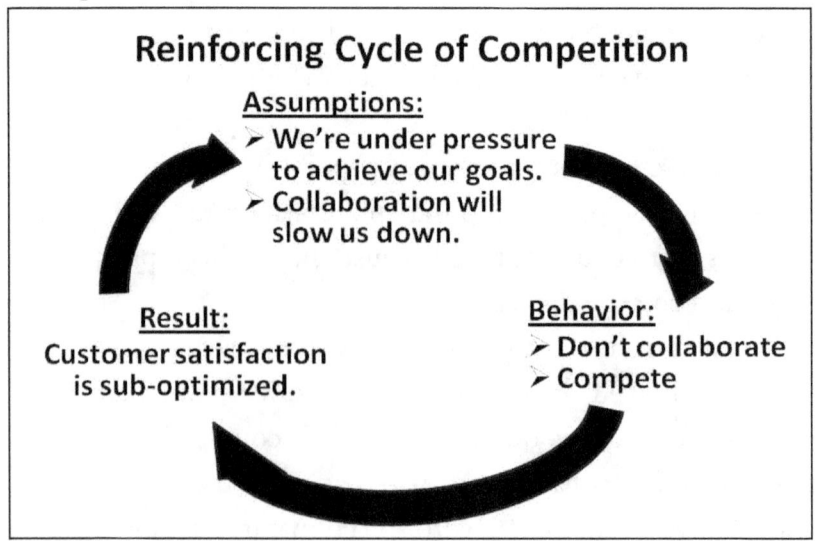

Figure 33-4

"Our Learning-to-Succeed exercise revealed that we can

better serve our customer by collaborating. Jacuzzi has proposed that the two teams of four become one team of eight. What do the rest of you think?"

"I'm for it," Aqua says. "We can significantly improve customer satisfaction."

Frostbite, Nitro, Geyser and Lagoon nod in agreement.

Celsius shakes his head. "I support becoming a team of eight. Eight is manageable. But in a few months we could have fifty penguins cutting ice blocks off this iceberg. In a year or two, we could have hundreds. Before Atlantis, I worked for a company that reorganized repeatedly in an attempt to bring employees with the needed skills together to address the problems of the day. It did not work. Employees formed competing teams, and reorganizations took so long to complete that new problems appeared. How can we deal with large teams?"

"Good question," Aristotle says. "Does anyone have any ideas?"

Jacuzzi nods. "I'd suggest we break the problem into two problems: training enough high performers and coordinating many teams."

"Good idea," Aristotle says. "If all employees are skilled in high performance, we can mix and match employees into any team size and composition. This approach will give us flexibility. We'll build a high-performance organization by building high-performance teams. We don't want a rigid organization that requires cumbersome reorganizations."

"I'll be happy to start a couple of one-page documents," Jacuzzi says. "Would anyone like to work with me?"

"I would," Celsius says. He turns to Aqua. "Aqua, can you help us? We're going to need someone who sees issues clearly and early."

"Sure," Aqua says, pleasantly surprised that Celsius sees her raising issues as a benefit."

"Please keep me in the loop on anything having to do with staffing and budgets," Aristotle says.

"Will do," Jacuzzi nods.

"How are you going to become one team of eight?" Aristotle asks.

"We can start by sharing best practices," Jacuzzi says. "Our process, experiments, and problems are well documented."

Frostbite turns to Aristotle. "Are you still managing the knowledge notebook?

"I've been too busy to give it any attention. Would you like to maintain the knowledge notebook for icebergs?"

"Yes, if someone will train me."

"I will," Fjord says. "I've been managing the knowledge notebook for the glacier business."

"Nitro," Jacuzzi says. "Can you prepare a maintenance plan for all the saws, conveyers, and handling equipment in the tankers that supports our increase in production?"

"You bet."

Jacuzzi continues: "Let's meet back here in one hour with all the documentation we currently have. Don't worry if it's rough. We have to start somewhere. We'll review what we have and start developing a comprehensive plan."

Aqua walks to the project milestone schedule "We have over a week to improve our ice cutting, conveying, and tanker loading processes. Can we review progress next week and decide if it makes sense to increase our September commitment?"

"That's a great idea," Fjord says.

Aristotle glances at the calendar on his phone. "How

about next Thursday morning, August 30 at eight o'clock?"

All the penguins nod.

Aristotle smiles. "You all have proven that high-performance teams are the best way to meet today's complex challenges. The contagious potential of high-performance teams makes collaborative behavior the lever that can move the world."

"I'm glad I gave collaboration a chance," Aqua says.

The end

Epilogue Summary

Aristotle assigned the highest performers from the glacier side of the company to the iceberg project. Although the team had no prior experience with icebergs, they quickly learned how to safely and reliably load much more ice in tankers than Aqua's team. The key is they spent nearly all their time repeating the Learn-Ideas-Test-Decide cycle.

By virtue of the advancements made by Jacuzzi's team, the September commitment far exceeded Hydro for Humanity's requirement and the project appeared to be very profitable. Aristotle no longer had to take out a loan, and he may be able reduce the price to help provide more water to customers faster.

The ensuing discussion concluded that high-performance teams achieve superior customer satisfaction and profit. Aqua captured this approach in a cycle that showed: build high-performance teams, solve complex problems, achieve superior customer satisfaction, and make enough money to pay the bills and build more high-performance teams.

Knowledge notebooks

Aristotle prepared knowledge notebooks containing information that can be used in the future to solve problems.

Jacuzzi's team solved the problem of ice blocks sliding in the tanker using the causal diagram in iceberg knowledge notebook that was created by Frostbite.

Aristotle pointed out that if colleagues don't trust the author of the knowledge notebook, the knowledge is not likely to be used.

Learning-to-Succeed

Aristotle conducted another Learning-to-Succeed exercise. Aqua, Celsius, Nitro and Frostbite learned the following:

1. Frostbite learned the power of visibility tools and processes.
2. Nitro learned that he has to trust the Learn-Ideas-Test-Decide cycle.
3. Celsius learned that high-performance teams can far outperform groups led by autocratic or participative leaders because high-performance teams rapidly complete learning cycles that solve problems, test assumptions, and develop better solutions.
4. Aqua learned that if she takes responsibility for everyone's success and helps resolve her colleagues' issues and worries, she can solve complex problems and satisfy customers.

ICEBERG DOWN: BUILDING HIGH-PERFORMANCE TEAMS

During the discussion, a model was created showing that high-performance teams require trust and visibility. Collaborative responsibility builds trust. Collaboration tools and processes are used to make problems and opportunities visible before, as well as after, important decisions are made.

Trust and visibility are required for teams to commit to a common purpose and ambitious goals. Aristotle defined a collaborating team as a team that improves performance primarily by integrating the best ideas from the team members.

In addition to integrating team members' best ideas, high-performance teams quickly and continually move through the Learn-Ideas-Test-Decide cycle, uncovering better solutions each time, until breakthroughs are found that create customer-valued innovation and new know-how. As a result, high-performance teams far exceed their goals.

Jacuzzi, Geyser, Fjord and Lagoon learned the following:

1. Geyser learned that he should have invited Aqua to the phone call with Hydro for Humanity because Aqua had a relationship with Meredith and would have made sure Meredith and Dalton knew about the sawdust solution to ice-block-slipping problem
2. Fjord learned that he should have invited Aqua, Celsius, Nitro and Frostbite to the brainstorming session to find solutions to the ice-blocks-sliding problem. He added that if he had, they would have found a better solution.
3. Lagoon learned that she should have enlisted Aqua, Celsius, Nitro and Frostbite's help on the ice-block-size experiments.
4. Jacuzzi learned that by not collaborating with Aqua,

Celsius, Nitro and Frostbite, the company missed its greatest opportunity to provide more water to Hydro for Humanity. She proposed that the two teams of four be combined into one team of eight.

High-performance organization

The ensuing discussion revealed that team members thought about collaborating with the other team. However, they assumed that they were under pressure to achieve their goals and that collaboration would slow their team down. Instead of collaborating, the two teams competed. Customer satisfaction was sub-optimized.

The Learning-to-Succeed exercise identified collaboration between teams as the greatest opportunity to improve customer satisfaction. All eight agreed to form one team, and a meeting was scheduled to develop a plan.

Celsius raised the issue of how to deal with a large team, since there could soon be dozens of employees cutting and conveying ice blocks off the iceberg.

Jacuzzi proposed breaking Celsius' issue into two problems: training enough high performers and coordinating many teams. Aristotle liked the idea because if all employees are skilled in high performance, employees can be mixed and matched into any team size and composition.

Aristotle called it a high-performance organization because it is made up of high-performance teams.

Aristotle summarized the power of high-performance teams by saying, "The contagious potential of high-performance teams makes collaborative behavior the lever that can move the world."

Leadership Comparison

Aristotle was everything Dr. Bond was not: He was not a world-renowned expert; he was not famous; he was not decisive; he didn't craft a catchy slogan; he didn't pass out buttons; he wasn't action-oriented; he didn't sacrifice customer satisfaction for short-term profit; and he didn't create a culture that doesn't tolerate problems, mistakes or excuses.

Instead, Aristotle saw his role as builder of high-performance teams. Aristotle maintained that role even though he was under pressure to deliver water. He did so because he knows that when facing complex problems in times of uncertainty, building high-performance teams offers the best chance of success.

How does Aristotle build high-performance teams?

First, Aristotle walks the talk. He admits mistakes. He takes responsibility for problems and for making everyone successful. He blames no one. By doing so, he creates a culture of trust, where it is safe to raise sensitive issues and try out collaborative behavior. By asking for ideas, problems were visible to all. Dr. Bond, however, asked only if projects were complete. His behavior kept problems hidden.

Second, Aristotle is a teacher. He teaches visibility tools. He devises exercises, such as Learning-to-Succeed, to learn and improve and obituaries to raise issues. He explains the difference between defensive responsibility and collaborative responsibility. He trains employees to follow the Learn-Ideas-Test-Decide cycle, prepare proposals, and solve problems.

Third, Aristotle is a coach. He is approachable on any topic. He pushes his employees to improve. He helps employees better understand their underlying assumptions and how defensive behavior is often based upon assumptions. He helps individuals see the destructive results of their defensive behavior, and he helps them develop new collaborative behaviors.

A comparison is shown in the following table.

	Dr. Hydrogen Bond	Aristotle Penguin
Role	Expert and decision maker.	Builder of high-performance teams.
Responsibility	Defensive: Aggressively defends himself and his ideas.	Collaborative: Takes responsibility for everyone's success and the project's success.
Breakthrough ideas	Relies upon himself.	Relies upon high-performance teams.
Strong leadership is:	1. Making quick decisions that lead to action. 2. Monitoring results. 3. Creating a culture where problems, mistakes, and excuses are not tolerated. 4. Clarifying desired outcomes. 5. Staying positive. 6. Telling employees they are part of something greater than themselves and that failure is not an option.	1. Finding ways to challenge and involve others. 2. Admitting mistakes. 3. Taking responsibility for problems. 4. Creating a culture of trust where it is safe to raise any issue, suggest any idea, and try new collaborative behavior. 5. Being approachable on any topic. 6. Teaching new tools and processes. 7. Coaching that makes everyone better.

Figure E-1

Glossary

A3s: Name given to Toyota's one-page documents. "A3" refers to paper size, which is approximately 11 inches by 17 inches. One-page documents are an effective collaboration and leadership tool. At Toyota, A3 practices standardize the process of problem solving, decision making, and innovation.[20]

Autocratic leader: Leader makes decision without seriously considering input. Autocratic leaderships is useful when decision-making speed is essential. Because autocratic leaders don't involve others, they often struggle to obtain buy-in on important decisions. Autocratic leaders often fail when they try to solve complex problems by themselves.

Agile development: Disciplined software development process that is particularly effective for complex software projects requiring collaboration. Agile development features iterative and incremental development to avoid the

GLOSSARY

high cost of discovering problems late in the development process. Requirements and solutions evolve through collaboration, preferably including customers.[6]

Cause-and-effect timeline: Timeline that shows the sequence and timing of decisions and results. Cause-and-effect timelines are used to identify which results were caused by which decisions. They are useful in gaining agreement regarding causes of problem, failures, and successes.

Causal diagrams: A graphical tool that shows the factors that contribute to a certain desired or undesired condition. In the story, the undesired condition was icebergs breaking. Two sets of factors existed: factors that contribute to iceberg strength and factors that contribute to stress. Causal diagrams are useful in identifying factors that contribute to, and detract from, customer satisfaction.

Collaborating team: Team members trust one another enough to raise issues, admit mistakes, ask for help, and share ideas and know-how. Team members make problems and opportunities visible and understandable before, as well as after, important decisions are made. Collaborating teams improve performance primarily by integrating the best ideas from the team members.

Collaboration tools and processes: Used to make problems and opportunities visible before, as well as after, important decisions are made. Examples include: wall charts, one-page documents, causal diagrams, fishbone diagrams, fault tree analysis, Five-Why analysis, cause-and-effect timelines, Obeya rooms, and trade-off curves.

Collaborative responsibility: Taking responsibility for the

GLOSSARY

success of colleagues and the success of the project. Several techniques were described in the story, including: Plussing, inquiring to understand, asking for ideas, and raising sensitive issues in private.

Confidence level: A measure of statistical reliability. A confidence level of 95 percent means there is a 95 percent chance that the actual population is within the confidence interval. A confidence interval may be greater than, less than, or an interval around a number. A voting survey may conclude that 40 percent of voters will vote for a candidate with a margin of error of 4 percent. Since a confidence level of 95 percent is typically used, this means there is a 95 percent probability that the number of people who will vote for a candidate is between 36 and 44 percent.

Cycle of reinforcing defensive behavior: Reinforcing dysfunctional cycle where an employee's non-flattering assumptions drive defensive behavior that leads colleagues to make non-flattering assumptions about that employee, leading to more defensive behavior. In the story, Aqua raised issues even when they sounded critical because she assumed Celsius made bad decisions. Because Aqua raised issues instead of just doing what she was asked, Celsius assumed Aqua was undependable, so he constantly reminded her to do what she was asked, which reinforced her assumption that Celsius made bad decisions.

Dysfunctional team: Team members understand problems and opportunities and rely upon each other for success, but there is insufficient trust to collaborate effectively. Management teams can be dysfunctional if managers are held individually accountable for results and individual results are more important than team results.

GLOSSARY

Individual accountability can promote defensive behavior that can defeat the changes managers know they need to make.

Five-Why analysis: Deductive reasoning root-cause analysis tool. The goal is to find the root causes, which when altered, solve the problem. The actual root causes are often hidden behind other causes. If the intermediate causes are altered the problem may go away for a while but will most likely reoccur. In each iteration the problem solver asks why the previous condition occurred until the root causes are revealed.

Knowledge notebooks: Collection of documents that represent what has been learned in a format that makes it reusable. Included are: reference material, rules of thumb, best practices, and relationships. Information in the knowledge notebooks can provide insight into solving new problems. Reviewing information in knowledge notebooks can be useful in the Learn step.

Lean: Management approach and practices aimed at maximizing customer value while eliminating waste. Waste is any activity that does not add value to the product or service sold to the customer. Seven wastes identified by Taiichi Ohno in *Toyota Production System: Beyond Large-Scale Production*: overproduction, waiting, inventory, defects, transportation, wasted motion, and waste in processing.

Learning-to-Succeed exercises: Group exercise designed to learn from experiences and figure out how to achieve better outcomes in the future. A goal of Learning-to-Succeed exercises is to make it safe to discuss sensitive and threatening issues including failures. It is typically two to four hours, with one or two breaks. Breaks provide participants with opportunities to synthesize what they have learned and figure out how to perform better.

Learn-Ideas-Test-Decide: Innovation-producing learning and decision-making cycle that produces better solutions each time a team makes a trip through the cycle.

High-performance organization: Organization made up of employees skilled in high performance. Employees can be mixed and matched into high-performance teams of any size and composition.

High-performance team: In addition to integrating team members' best ideas, high-performance teams quickly and continually move through the Learn-Ideas-Test-Decide cycle, uncovering better solutions each time, until breakthroughs are found that create customer-valued innovation and new know-how. As a result, high-performance teams far exceed their goals. It's also usually fun. A difference between collaborating teams and high-performance teams is that high-performance teams have enough trust and visibility to continually and quickly complete Learn-Ideas-Test-Decide cycles. Collaborating teams usually require encouragement to repeat the cycle. Without encouragement, collaborating teams are more likely to integrate team members best ideas and move into implementation, when another quick trip or two through the cycle would produce a much better solution.

Obeya **room:** *Obeya* means big room in Japanese. Lean practices are often performed in *Obeya* room. In organizations that practice Lean, *Obeya* rooms are used for strategy development, product development, and solving

GLOSSARY

complex problems. Wall charts are commonly used so entire teams can understand problems and opportunities and to promote collaboration.

Participative leader: Leader solicits input before making decisions. Because group members are involved in making decisions, participative leaders usually receive more decision buy-in than autocratic leaders. Because it is safe to raise issues, offer dissenting ideas, admit mistakes, or ask for help, participative leaders have a better chance of adapting to changing conditions than autocratic leaders..

Proposal: Solution to a problem. Proposal contents typically include: background, current condition, objectives, analysis, alternatives for implementation, issues that must be resolved and assumption the proposal relies upon to succeed, and implementation plan.

Six Sigma: Strategies, techniques, and tools for process improvement. Six sigma is a statistical term referring to a process that generates a maximum of 3.4 defective parts per million (PPM) when the amount of process shifts are less than ± 1.5 standard deviations from the mean (average). Lean Six Sigma combines Lean and Six Sigma. Design for Six Sigma (DFSS) is a product development technique that determines the needs of customers and the business, and drives those needs into the development of new products.

Smile-and-nod meetings: Meeting in which the leader patronizes the attendees and controls the outcome. Attendees are supposed to smile and nod on cue, to indicate their agreement with everything the leader says. The disadvantages of smile-and-nod meetings are: issues and dissenting ideas are suppressed, which can reduce organizational performance and cause failure, and job security and career advancement can depend more upon smiling and nodding in meetings than job performance.

Strategy: Collection of decisions that together promise to achieve a desired vision and goals. It is during strategy development that the most important questions facing organizations are answered, including:
1. For what purpose does our organization exist?
2. What is our vision for the future?
3. What are our short term goals or mission?
4. In which businesses will we compete?
5. Which markets and customers will we serve?
6. Which products and services will we develop?
7. Where and how will we develop and manufacture our products?
8. How will we fill customer orders?
9. How will we service customers?
10. How will we obtain investment dollars and funding?

Team: Two or more individuals committed to a common purpose or mission and who rely upon each other for success. Because the roles on a team are interdependent, team members share responsibility for success.

Trade-off curves: Graphical description of the performance limits of two or more key parameters. Trade-off curves enable the development of product and process designs that won't fail, and drive designs toward optimality. Trade-off curves also provide a baseline upon which to improve product and process performance and focus research and continuous improvement efforts, [16]

GLOSSARY

Toyota: Company whose practices are the basis for Lean. In the 1980s and 1990s, Toyota dominated the competitive auto industry by introducing Lexus (1989) and Prius (1997), and consistently leading all companies in quality and customer satisfaction. In the 2000's, Toyota's priorities shifted to market share and profit growth. By the late 2000s, recalls and excess inventory resulted in: market share loss, the company's first financial loss in seventy years, and loss of credibility. Toyota is working to regain its reputation for superior customer satisfaction.

Notes

1. Nearly 900 million people have no access to clean water, and 2.5 billion don't have a safe way to dispose of human waste. These conditions result in the death of nearly 10,000 people every day, mostly children under the age of five. Rosenberg, Tina. "The Burden of Thirst." *National Geographic.* 102. April 2010.
2. The phrase "smile-and-nod meeting" is drawn from author's experience. An excellent book on control tactics of managers is *Flawed Advice and Management Traps* by Chris Argyrus.
3. Ohno, Taiichi. *Toyota Production System: Beyond Large-Scale Production.* Portland, Oregon: Productivity Inc. 1988.
4. For an excellent discussion on how assumptions impact strategy, see *The Lean Startup* by Eric Ries.
5. Learn-Ideas-Test-Decide was derived from over thirty-years of experience solving problems.
    a. Learn-Ideas-Test-Decide draws upon Kepner-Tregoe problem-solving-and-decision-making process. Kepner-Tregoe has three main steps: problem analysis, decision analysis, and potential problem analysis. I found the potential problem analysis step very useful, in fact, too

NOTES

useful. Potential problems were often serious enough that I had to go back through decision analysis, which was unpopular with people who thought I should have gotten it right the first time. I found Failure Mode and Effect Analysis (FMEA) can have the same challenge because FMEA is usually performed after important decisions are made. It's essential that solutions to problems associated with alternative decisions and assumptions the decisions rely upon to succeed are tested before important decisions are made.

    b. Learn-Ideas-Test-Decide draws upon LAMDA (Look, Ask, Model, Discuss, and Act) developed by Dr. Allen Ward to describe how Toyota's engineers solve problems. LAMDA is a learning cycle performed in each problem-solving step: problem description, root cause analysis, evaluation of alternatives, and implementation.

    c. Learn-Ideas-Test-Decide draws upon Six Sigma.

    d. Learn-Ideas-Test-Decide draws from Agile software development. Agile relies upon rapid learning cycles and frequent integration to avoid the high cost of discovering defects late in the development process. An excellent book is *Leading Lean Software Development: Results Are not the Point* by Mary and Tom Poppendieck.

6. Ordonez, Lisa D., Schweitzer, Maurice E., Galinsky, Adam D., Bazerman, Max H. "Goals Gone Wild: The Systemic Side Effects of Over-Prescribing Goal Setting" 2009.

7. Poppendieck, Mary, Poppendieck, Tom, *Leading Lean Software Development: Results Are not the Point*. Boston, MA: Addison-Wesley. 2009.

8. Toyota calls these exercises *hansei*, which means reflection. The phrase Learning-to-Succeed is borrowed from Spear, Steven. *The High-Velocity Edge*. United States: McGraw-Hill, 2009.

9. Perutz, Max, *I Wish I'd Made You Angry Earlier*, Oxford, Great Britain: Oxford University Press. 2002.

10. Water Conflict Chronology List. URL: http//www.worldwater.org/conflict/list [18 December 2013]

NOTES

11. Inspired by Paul Levy's articles on Mad Emperor's Disease and egophrenia.
12. Wall charts in conference rooms are part of Toyota's *Obeya* approach. *Obeya* is a Japanese word that means big room. Toyota first used Obeya practices on Prius to successfully integrate research into Prius vehicle development. *Obeya* rooms have gained significant popularity for product development, project management, operations management, and status reporting, among other uses.
13. Bridges, William. *Managing Transitions: Making the Most of Change*. Reading, MA: Corporate & Professional Publishing Group, 1991.
14. Lehrer, Jonah. *Imagine*. New York, New York: Houghton Mifflin Harcourt Publishing Company, 2012.
15. Inspired by author's experience and drawn from Argyrus, Chris. *Flawed Advice and Management Traps*. New York, New York: Oxford University Press, 2000. and Senge, Peter. *The Fifth Discipline*. United States: Doubleday, 2006
16. Weightman, Gavin. *The Frozen Water Trade*. New York, New York: Hyperion, 2003.
17. Discussion on trust is drawn from author's experience. Two excellent books on teams are: *Smart Trust: Creating Prosperity, Energy, and Joy in a Low-Trust World* by Stephen M.R. Covey, Greg Link and Rebecca Link, and *The Speed of Trust: The One Thing that Changes Everything* by Stephen M.R. Covey.
18. Ward, Allen C. *Lean Product and Process Development*. Cambridge, MA: Lean Enterprise Institute, 2007 and Kennedy, Michael, Harmon, Kent, Minnock, Ed. *Ready, Set, Dominate*, Richmond, Virginia, The Oaklea Press, 2008.
19. Discussion on teams is drawn from author's experience. Two excellent books on teams are *The Wisdom of Teams* by Jon Katzenbach and Douglas Smith, and *Overcoming the Five Dysfunctions of a Team* by Patrick Lencioni.
20. Two excellent books on A3 thinking and process are *A3 Thinking* by Durward Sobek and Art Smalley, and *Managing to Learn* by John Shook.

About the Author

Ed Minnock is founder and CEO of Ed Minnock and Associates, a consulting firm that specializes in helping teams reach their high-performance potential.

Ed has broad experience as an executive, a Lean Product Development consultant, and a practitioner of the Toyota Way. He has built and led business teams, strategy development teams, product development teams, manufacturing teams, and task teams. He has built and led teams that have turned businesses around.

Before founding Ed Minnock and Associates, Ed worked at Targeted Convergence Corporation, where he trained three thousand people in Lean Product Development and Lean Problem Solving.

Ed's experience includes Hewlett Packard, where he was a vice president and general manager, responsible for two businesses, with revenue of nearly a billion dollars. Other positions at Hewlett Packard included director of

ABOUT THE AUTHOR

research and development, and director of manufacturing. Before Hewlett Packard, he worked for successful start-up technology companies.

Ed earned a BS degree in Industrial Engineering and Operations Research from Cornell University and an MBA from Colorado State University.

Ed lives with his wife and daughter in Colorado.

For more information about building high-performance teams or to contact Ed Minnock, please visit www.edminnockandassociates.com

www.ingramcontent.com/pod-product-compliance
Lightning Source LLC
Chambersburg PA
CBHW051634170526
45167CB00001B/180